Teaching Travel Tourism 14+

Cliff Huggett and Deborah Pownall

Open University Press

Open University Press
McGraw-Hill Education
McGraw-Hill House
Shoppenhangers Road
Maidenhead
Berkshire
England
SL6 2QL

email: enquiries@openup.co.uk
world wide web: www.openup.co.uk

and Two Penn Plaza, New York, NY 10121-2289, USA

First published 2010

A catalogue record of this book is available from the British Library

ISBN-13: 978-0-33-523826-2 (pb) 978-0-33-523827-9 (hb)
ISBN-10: 0335238262 (pb) 0335238270 (hb)

Library of Congress Cataloging-in-Publication Data
CIP data applied for

Typeset by RefineCatch Limited, Bungay, Suffolk
Printed in the UK by CPI Antony Rowe, Chippenham, Wiltshire

Fictitious names of companies, products, people, characters and/or data that
may be used herein (in case studies or in examples) are not intended to
represent any real individual, company, product or event.

The **McGraw·Hill** Companies

Contents

Figures

Series editor's preface

For historical reasons perhaps, subject pedagogy for Post 16 teachers has not been considered a professional development priority. The possession of appropriate academic or vocational qualifications and experience have traditionally been considered sufficient for those teaching older students assumed themselves to possess the motivation and skills for effective learning. However, the increasing numbers of 14–16 year olds taking part of their programmes in FE colleges, the rise in the participation rate of 16–19 year olds and the increasing number of 18–30 year olds having experience of higher education, have created a large and diverse population in all sector institutions presenting a challenge to those teaching Post 14 students. Both the 2003 and 2006 Ofsted surveys of Post 16 teacher training and the 2007 reforms of initial teacher training and continuing professional development, have drawn attention to the urgent need for both new and existing teachers to receive training to teach their subject or curriculum specialism and to receive support from subject coaches or mentors in the workplace. Most of the programmes preparing the 40,000 trainees annually to teach in the lifelong learning sector are generic in nature, rather than subject specific.

Partly because of the Institute for Learning's requirements regarding both CPD and professional formation, there is considerable growth in in-service continuing professional development and, given the attention given by both Ofsted and DCSF to subject pedagogy as described above, it is likely that there will be a sharp CPD focus for many colleges on subject teaching, particularly since much of the burden of subject based training will fall on the shoulders of FE college based mentors. The increase in vocational education in schools, particularly with the introduction of diplomas, will see a growing need for secondary PGCE students and existing 14–18 secondary teachers to enhance their subject pedagogy for 14+ students. One of the key recommendations of a recent report on vocational teacher training* is that "Vocational and applied pedagogies should become a research priority and be embedded within school, further education (FE) and higher education (HE) initial teacher training (ITT) and continuing professional development (CPD)."

* The Skills Commission (2010) *An Inquiry into Teacher training in Vocational Education* London: The Skills Commission P.14

Each series title is therefore aimed to act as support for teachers, whether on a formal initial or CPD programme or simply as a guide for those teaching the subject on a daily basis in one of a variety of possible contexts: secondary, FE, Adult and Community Education, work-based training. Chapters in each title follow a similar format. Chapter 1 deals with the nature of subject(s) in the curriculum area, considering any contesting conceptions of what the subject should be about, as well as current issues connected with teaching it. There is a focus on subject updating, identifying recent key developments in subjects as well as the means for students to be able to update themselves. Chapter 2 provides an introduction to the major programmes in the subject area focussing mainly on those in the National Qualifications Framework such as GCSE, AS, Key Skills, NVQ, Diplomas, although reference is made to the Framework for Higher Education Qualifications. There is a consideration of the central features of each programme such as aims and objectives, unitisation or modularity, content. The chapter also guides readers in the task of turning syllabus into learning via schemes of work. The third chapter considers key skills and functional skills, looking at differing models of skills development and how such skills might be taught through the subject. Chapter 4 looks at the teaching and learning strategies most often used in the curriculum area. There are clearly certain learning and teaching strategies that are used universally across post 14 programmes – lectures, discussion, presentations are the most obvious. Even these, however, will need to be treated in the context of their use in the subject area. Presentations which model those in advertising or marketing might be effective learning strategies in an AS Media Studies or Applied Business GCSE, whereas in Key Skills Communications they might have the purpose of developing oracy skills and as part of an Access course of developing study skills. Chapter 5 considers resources as used in the context of the curriculum area. When audio-visual resources are being considered, for example, students might be presented with exemplar handouts and PowerPoint presentations with subject-related content. ICT resources should be considered in terms of their strengths in relation to the subject. Are there good commercial software packages, for example? How can they best be used for teaching? What are the key web sites relating to the subject area? How might searching best be carried out? There is a consideration of the range of published resources available in the subject area, with examples of how material is presented and how use of it is structured. Chapter 6 offers guidance on the role of the teacher as assessor in the programmes identified in Chapter 2, with a particular emphasis on the range of assessment strategies used as part of these programmes.

Each title features a range of pedagogical features which might be useful alone, in pairs or in groups. Readers are invited for example to reflect, discuss, respond to a range of visual stimuli, give short answer responses to questions, consider case studies, complete short tasks.

Travel and tourism are areas of the national and global economy which have grown dramatically in recent years. In the UK alone, tourism is estimated to be worth £75 billion and employ 2.6 million people. These areas comprise a vast array of occupational roles described by Cliff Huggett and Deborah Pownall, from business management to professional to maintenance roles, so that teaching and training those who work within or intend to enter this sector is particularly challenging for the teacher. However, learning about both travel and tourism is not necessarily narrowly vocational and the authors indicate clearly how such learning can be more broadly educative and develop a wide range of skills, knowledge and understanding. In doing so, Huggett and Pownall draw on their considerable experience both as teachers and teacher trainers, as well as the good practice and range of methodologies demonstrated by many excellent teachers.

Andy Armitage

Preface

Returning to the office after a long day teaching leisure and tourism students on our 14–19 Postgraduate Certificate of Education (PGCE) programme, I was bemoaning the fact that there were no textbooks that addressed the specific pedagogical issues relating to the subject to back up my own teaching. 'Then write one!' said the Head of Department, Andy Armitage, now editor for this series of texts on the pedagogy of vocational subjects. Two or three years later, after steadily trying to avoid the commitment, the idea became a reality.

Although I started my teaching career as a physical educationist, I questioned the accepted pedagogies of my subject from the beginning, and this interest in pedagogical studies has always underpinned my career. From those early years of teaching in schools I moved into the further education sector and it was here that I developed an interest more specifically in curriculum development. My first brush with travel and tourism was in teaching on Business and Technical Education Council (BTEC) National Leisure and Tourism programmes and, later, through establishing General National Vocational Qualification (GNVQ) programmes.

There was really nobody to advise me how to teach travel and tourism, although I did realize the potential of the subject to motivate learners. My experience of pedagogical method, however, was enhanced when I became first a moderator for BTEC Nationals and then for GNVQs. This took me into a wide variety of colleges and schools around the country and, of course, I was able to make contact with, and draw on the experience of, a large number of teachers of travel and tourism.

With yet another stroke of good fortune, late in my career, I was invited to teach at Canterbury first on PGCE programmes and later on a wider range. So I found a voice, at last, for my passion for the study of pedagogy, unconstrained by subject boundaries. In truth, this interests me more than my subject specialism, but teaching on our 14–19 PGCE programme brought together those two areas of my history: the years as a teacher of leisure and tourism in further education, and the pedagogical studies and teaching of my latter years.

As an examiner at John Moore's University, I met Deborah Pownall who was leading the 14–19 PGCE programme for the teaching of travel and tourism. It was because of her wealth of experience both in the industry and as a teacher of the subject that I invited her to co-write this publication with me. Thus, it is also a reflection of that experience and of her perceptions of how best to teach travel and tourism.

We have seen good practice and excellent interactive methodologies practised by many excellent teachers, and it is this that we wish to share with the reader. This publication is designed to create a link between the subject matter, on which there is a vast array of publications, and the theories about the way we teach it: the pedagogy of travel and tourism. It is intended to be a support for those subject specialists embarking on initial teaching training and perhaps a reference for those already practising but, as much as anything, it is hoped that it will act as a stimulus to further reading.

We do realize that those reading this book may be very well qualified in the subject and have considerable experience, but we have chosen to begin by giving an overview of what you need to know in order to teach travel and tourism. Certainly, as a subject it has its detractors in educational circles, and we have tried to address this by pointing out just how important travel and tourism has become in our society today. This then leads us to look at the various programmes that are available to those who want to follow a career in the industry, and then to share with you our experiences of teaching the subject.

We are sure that there will be many of our readers who have, themselves, valuable experiences to share in the same way. We hope that this book will still help you in some way, perhaps, to structure those experiences, but we would also like to hear from you so that we can all continue to grow and learn more about this subject which we have been lucky enough to be able to turn into a career.

Cliff Huggett

Acknowledgements

The authors would like to thank all those who have helped and advised us in the preparation of this book. This certainly includes our colleagues in the Post-compulsory Department at Canterbury Christ Church University and the Faculty of Education, Community and Leisure at Liverpool John Moore's University.

I am particularly appreciative of those who advised me on the chapter on key and functional skills, Jo-Ann Delaney, Amanda Cope and Jane Evershed. They helped me to realize that the importance of embedding the development of the skills into our everyday teaching cannot be underestimated and that, as educators, it is something for which we all share a responsibility. Catherine Carden, tutor for the 14–19 PGCE Travel and Tourism programme, has given valuable advice and resources. But the encouragement I have received and the discussions that I have had with others, such Andy Armitage, Head of Department and editor of the series, and Gina Donovan, have been invaluable, particularly in those moments of despair when we thought that the project was impossible.

Deborah, also, is equally appreciative towards her colleagues who have willingly lent her both their time and resources, some of which appear in the book as exemplar materials. In particular, she would like to thank Carol Prescott of Liverpool John Moore's University, Robbie Leith of Liverpool Community College, Zoey Slater of the Blackpool Sixth Form College and Gill Duglan.

Finally, of course, we would both like to thank those close to us, family and friends who have had to endure our frustrations and long periods of neglect of them, and who, nevertheless, have encouraged us and supported us throughout the project.

Figure 6.3 is reproduced from *Classroom Activities for AQA GCSE Leisure & Tourism* (Catherine Carden: ISBN 9780956268020) with permission of Travel & Tourism Publishing Ltd.

Abbreviations

ABTA	Association of British Travel Agents
ABTAC	ABTA Travel Agency Certificate
ADS	autistic spectrum disorder
AITO	Association of Independent Tour Operators
ALAN	Adult Literacy and Numeracy
ATOL	Air Travel Organizers' Licence
AVCE	Advanced Vocational Certificate in Education
BATA	British Air Transport Association
BEC	Business Education Council
BIS	Department for Business, Innovation and Skills
BTEC	Business and Technical Education Council
CAA	Civil Aviation Authority
CPD	continued professional development
DCMS	Department of Culture, Media and Sport
DCSF	Department for Children, Schools and Families
DfES	Department for Education and Skills
DMO	destination marketing organization
EBP	Education Business Partnership
ECM	Every Child Matters
EMA	Educational Maintenance Allowance
FDA	Foundation Degree in Arts
FE	further education
GCSE	General Certificate of Secondary Education
GNVQ	General National Vocational Qualifications
GTC	General Teaching Council
HE	higher education
HNC	Higher National Certificate
HND	Higher National Diploma
ICT	information and communication technology
IfL	Institute for Learning
ILM	Institute of Leadership and Management

ILP	Individual Learning Plan
IT	information technology
NIACE	National Institute of Adult and Continuing Education
NOCN	National Open College Network
NQCF	National Qualifications Credit Framework
NQF	National Qualifications Framework
NVQ	National Vocational Qualification
OCN	Open College Network
Ofsted	Office for Standards in Education
PGCE	Postgraduate Certificate of Education
PLTS	personal learning and thinking skills
QCA	Qualifications and Curriculum Authority
QCDA	Qualifications and Curriculum Development Agency
QCF	Qualifications and Credit Framework
RDA	regional development agency
ROSPA	Royal Society for the Prevention of Accidents
SNVQ	Scottish National Vocational Qualifications
TDA	Teachers Development Agency
TEC	Technical Education Council
UCAS	Universities and Colleges Admissions Services
UKSP	UK Skills Passport
VLE	virtual learning environment
YA	Young Apprenticeships

1

The context of the travel and tourism curriculum and related issues

In this chapter we will be looking at:

- travel and tourism as a subject of study
- concepts of travel and tourism
- working in travel and tourism
- the knowledge, understanding and skills required to work in the various sectors
- the organization of the industry
- teaching and learning in the travel and tourism curriculum
- how learning programmes are affected by national and local initiatives
- the profiles of learners on travel and tourism programmes
- how the industry has been affected by changing technologies, dynamic packaging, greener transport and security post-9/11.

Introduction

'The study of tourism uncovers new ways of seeing tourism, maps out new concepts, elaborates new theories and builds up a body of knowledge' (Tribe 2005: 49).

In his paper on 'Tourism, knowledge and the curriculum', John Tribe (2005) discusses the growing interest in the study of the phenomenon of tourism, and comes to the conclusion that it 'is . . . essentially much less than the activity it describes'. Although his concern was chiefly with the academic study of tourism, we can surely follow his argument to reach the conclusion that, at all levels of study, there is an intrinsic value in the subject. This chapter explores those concepts further as we introduce the reader to the breadth and depth of the travel and tourism curriculum and the learners who will potentially populate our classrooms.

As every graduate student of travel and tourism knows, the industry has been part of our cultural heritage, probably since we took our first faltering steps as upright biped beings exploring our local neighbourhoods. Today, of, course, this has grown into a multi-billion pound/dollar/euro/yen industry that even the threat of international recession cannot eclipse. Still we are filled with the desire to discover and experience other cultures, and corporate businesses can hardly survive unless they are prepared to travel the world.

In this chapter we intend to remind readers of the vast scope of the travel and tourism industry; you examine the possibilities for employment and concomitant skills and knowledge that are necessary to fill these roles as a prelude to considering the impact of all this on the teaching and learning of travel and tourism as a curriculum subject.

It is, of course, possible that many of our readers will have studied the following topics already at an academic level, but this publication is intended to reach a number of people, some of whom may have little knowledge of the industry, so it is hoped that this brief introduction will convince them of the importance of our subject as an element of the curriculum. For those who are already well informed perhaps it will serve as a reminder of what the subject is all about and as a stimulus to considering how best to engage their learners in its complexities.

Travel and tourism as a subject of study

Why are travel and tourism important?

Travel and tourism have been part of human leisure activity possibly since we started to form social groupings. Evidence of the first travel guides can be found in ancient times; the first Olympic games were held in Greece in 776 BC; the Middle Ages saw travel to the Holy Land, and the European 'Grand Tour' marked the Renaissance and Reformation eras. The students of today may only think about modern tourism, however, exploring history through tourism is a way of placing this global industry in its historic perspective.

In today's society travelling has become a defining feature of many people's non-work activity, especially in the developed Western culture, while travel to significant destinations remains an important part of many world religions. Global travel has become more accessible to all classes through modern transport; the economic value of tourism has grown exponentially over the past 60 years and seems to hold no boundaries, as indicated by Virgin Galactic offering space travel. Tourism has become an integral part of many countries' economies. In the UK, the travel and tourism industry is recognized as a generator of economic wealth, falling within the Department for Culture, Media and Sport (DCMS):

> Tourism is one of the largest industries in the UK, with direct tourism spending accounting for 2.7% of UK Gross Value Added, or approximately £86.3 billion in 2007, comprising: spend by overseas residents amounted to 16 billion pounds in 2007, whilst UK transport carriers commanded fares to the value of 2.7 billion pounds; Domestic tourist spent 21.2 billion pounds on trips of more than one night and 45.4 billion on day trips.
>
> (http://www.tourismtrade.org.uk/MarketIntelligenceResearch/ KeyTourismFacts.asp, accessed 23 Feb. 2010)

The festivals and events industry has seen dramatic growth through major international events such as the Olympics and the Football World Cup, each one used to regenerate cities (Richards 2007). We now see music festivals that attract European-wide attendance. Holidays are planned around major events such as cricket or rugby tours. The DCMS (2005) policy document *Winning: A Tourism Strategy for 2012 and Beyond*, has identified that the hosting of the Olympic Games in 2012 will be a major boost to the tourism industry in the UK, increasing employment and interest in the subject, we hope, over the coming years. The economic value of the industry is by no means confined to the UK, and the people we teach may be involved with a worldwide industry. The World Tourism Organization records: 'In 2008, international tourist arrivals grew by 2% to reach 924 million, up 16 million over 2007. International tourism generated US$ 856 billion (€ 625 billion) in 2007, or 30% of the world's exports of services. 1.6 billion forecast international tourist arrivals worldwide by 2020' (http://www.unwto.org/index.php).

To allow the facts and figures such as those given above to be comparable between and within countries, some understanding and agreement has to be reached about the concepts of the industry. Although it may seem to be obvious, what do we mean when we talk about travel and tourism?

Reflection 1.1

Consider five reasons why you think that travel and tourism are important in today's society.

Concepts of the tourist, tourism and travel

There have been numerous attempts to define tourism with the World Travel Organization taking the lead. They have defined tourism as:

> activities of persons travelling to and staying in places outside their usual environment for not more than one consecutive year for leisure, business and other purposes not related to the exercise of an activity remunerated from within the place visited. The use of this broad concept makes it possible to identify tourism between countries as well as tourism within a country. 'Tourism' refers to all activities of visitors, including both 'tourists' (overnight visitors) and 'same-day visitors'.
> (www.world-tourism.org cited in Page 2007)

The tourist is defined (in part to enable economic measurement of the industry) as persons staying more than 24 hours away from home and less than a year, though the purpose of their visit also impacts on this definition. Page (2007) also relates to 'travel', what Leiper (1995) describes as the transit route carrying outbound and inbound tourists to the destination, which is at the heart of tourism (Figure 1.1). The study of, and employment in, transportation that meets the needs of all populations, in addition to the tourist need, is an important area of study in tourism.

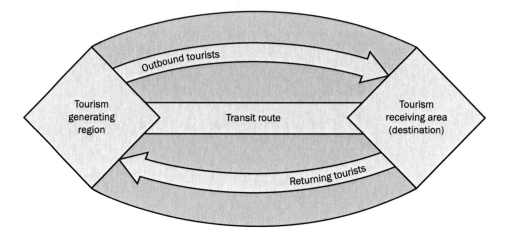

Figure 1.1 Leiper's model (redrawn from Page 1995; based on and modified from Leiper 1990, in Page 2007)

Tourism and the environment

The industry, while being so vast, influences many aspects of the environment in which it operates. In many cases this can be to the benefit of that environment. Tourist attractions, such as Cornwall's Eden project which has been developed on a former industrial site, have been of benefit both economically and environmentally to a number of areas. As tour operators look for different destinations, new overseas destinations, such as Cape Verde on the West African coast, have developed owing to the opportunities offered to remote places to become involved in tourism.

Furthermore, low-cost airlines flying into new smaller airports provide a much needed stimulus to those local economies.

However, where travel and tourism is poorly managed, it can cause much damage to cultures, environments and heritage. Unfortunately, there are many examples from around the world of such issues surrounding tourism. Hopefully, the study of travel and tourism will enable your learners to ensure that the impact of the industry is a positive one.

Tourism, then, can be controversial and there are a great many case studies available to support the teaching of tourism. Chapter 6 suggests sources for both background reading and teaching materials.

Reflection 1.2

Can you name five areas that have suffered and five that benefited through tourism?

Studying travel and tourism

The size, economic and social importance of the industry should indicate that it deserves serious study, but we should add to this the numbers of people employed in travel and tourism. The *National Skills Strategy for England* (there are similar documents for Wales, Ireland and Scotland) produced by People 1st (2007) records that the wider industry of hospitality, leisure, travel and tourism was worth £75 billion to the UK economy in 2007. Furthermore, as Deloitte observes: 'in 2007 the tourism sector supported over 2.6 million jobs; 1.4 million directly and a further 1.3 million indirectly. Jobs directly supported by tourism account for 4.3% of all employment, and the combination of direct and indirect employment is equivalent to 8.4% of all jobs' (http://www.tourismtrade.org.uk/MarketIntelligence Research/KeyTourism Facts.asp, accessed 14 Jan. 2010). These figures give a view of how such an important industry does impact on all society. Therefore, it also deserves that its people be knowledgeable, trained and developed in a structured manner. The programmes you will be asked to teach are central to this proposition.

Travel and tourism is a multidisciplinary subject which means that it has a wide range of subjects complementing its study, subjects such as environmental issues, sociology, geography and economics. The study of travel and tourism does not have an overarching academic agreement on how to approach the subject. The study of a subject that touches everyone's lives through participation in their non-work time seems to invite comment and views from all. This allows you, as the teacher, to adopt a perspective that suits the curriculum and the learners' needs.

The vast range of programmes and qualifications you may encounter in your teaching are discussed in Chapter 2. This all contributes to the enjoyment of teaching a subject that not only can have a major impact on society, but is also diverse, informative and colourful. Indeed, it has many aspects that should capture any student's imagination, no matter what their interest. As a teacher, or programme developer, you should have an understanding of the range and depth of the industry as a subject of study. The next section covers the range of occupational roles found in the sector and then the skills, knowledge and understanding needed to fulfil them.

Working in the travel and tourism industry

The range of job roles within the industry is immense and the people we teach will find jobs and careers all over the world. New areas of employment are opening up. Our learners will see a different tourism industry in the future, as can be seen from the example below about the growth of the cruise industry, a very different looking sector from 20 years ago.

More than 12.6 million people sailed on cruise ships in 2008. While the cruise industry continues to grow, it requires more and more staff to work on board the cruise ships and people of all nationalities are being recruited to do these cruise jobs. At this time, there are over 40 new cruise ships on order for delivery between now and 2012.

(https://www.cruiseservices.co.uk/the-cruise-industry.html, accessed 19 Feb. 2010)

Our travel and tourism industries, then, represent all types of business, from the local restaurant owner to the multinational hotel corporation; from the seaside fairground to the giant theme park; from the village museum to the stately home; from the local mini-bus company to the major airlines. Their scope encompasses guest houses and public houses, caravan parks and holiday lets, tour operators and conference organizers.

However, it must be remembered that the public sector also provides many tourist attractions, such as local authority-run historic buildings, galleries and museums, and are also responsible for transportation networks, clearly involving a wide range of possible occupations. National government regulates and licenses many areas of tourism and travel; they also drive strategy, as has been mentioned earlier. Organizations such as English Heritage are partly funded by tax payers, but are major contributor to the tourism industry in England. Likewise similar organizations exist in Wales and Scotland and Ireland.

Organizations in the voluntary sector also provide many tourist attractions, such as the National Trust which manages over 350 properties, plus forests, woods, fens, beaches, farmland, downs, moorland, islands, archaeological remains, castles, nature reserves and villages.

The setting up of sector skills councils in 2002, led to many debates surrounding what should and should not be included when trying to define the industry. Museums and retail, which are integral to the 'city tourism' offer, are not in the People 1st Sector Skills Council's footprint; however, you would not exclude them from your teaching of products and services of a destination. Further, national parks or a place of worship, such as a cathedral, all have a dual purpose but are, in *the public's mind*, part of the tourism industry. These organizations may support and benefit from tourism, yet planning for and dealing with tourists is not their primary role, placing tension between their differing roles. Each organization has to balance these juxtapositions of their daily life. You can see how difficult it is to apply strict definitions to the industry and perhaps how the interests of the various sub-sectors and, indeed, the interests of other industries such as sport and retail might overlap. The People 1st footprint of 14 sub-sectors may be found in Figure 1.2.

• Contract food service providers	• Membership clubs
• Events	• Pubs, bars and nightclubs
• Gambling	• Restaurants
• Holiday parks	• Self-catering accommodation
• Hospitality services	• Tourist services
• Hostels	• Travel services
• Hotels	• Visitor attractions

Figure 1.2 The People 1st Sector Skills Council 'footprint' of industry sub-sectors

There are many texts that can provide fuller descriptions and discussions on this topic; some are listed in the appendices. We will discuss this later in this chapter too.

Reflection 1.3

Think about other organizations related to tourism but which do not have tourism as their primary role and list the areas of tension that might be found within that organization.

With such a variety of environments, what kinds of occupations and activities can our learners expect to engage in when working in the industry?

Clearly, from the foregoing discussion, there will be a very wide variety of things they might do: from providing customer service in a local tourist attraction, to becoming a multi-lingual tour guide at a historical location; from selling holidays to the public, to scoping future potential of new holiday resorts; they might be employed as ground staff at an airport, or even air traffic control. There is a wide range of levels at which travel and tourism employment can be found. This range extends from 'front-line' staff (such as resort reception, travel agency consultants, call centre operatives and catering), through middle management roles (for example day-to-day supervision of front-line operations), to senior management, strategic planning and decision-making roles at a high level in both private and public organizations. People 1st and Springboard UK have formed a further organization, UK Skills Passport (UKSP), to map out the job opportunities. Their interactive career map is a helpful source to explain the industry. This can be accessed at http://www.uksp.co.uk/CareerMap.aspx.

You will be required to understand, and teach, the roles found in the industry and their interrelated nature. To do so, you need to understand the nature of employment within the travel and tourism industry: its seasonality; the commitment to part-time and shift work; the unsociable hours, teamwork and customer focus; and the training and progression routes.

Skills, knowledge and understanding for the travel and tourism industry

Reflection 1.4

Almost every city centre has a 4-star hotel with multiple activities in its 'product offer': accommodation; restaurant; spa; leisure and fitness suite; conference and event services.

List the range of jobs that you think might be required to run the hotel efficiently.

From your reflections, what skills, knowledge and understanding would your learners need to develop to fulfil these roles competently? Here are some suggestions categorized under the headings of the various areas of responsibility:

Business management – strategic planning, finance, marketing, customer service, managing human and physical resources, legal obligations.
Professional – health and safety, chef skills, food preparation, fitness training, event management, managing booking systems.
Maintenance – of premises and equipment, health and safety.

While teaching very vocationally focused programmes is one area on the spectrum of travel and tourism teaching, you must not forget that, as educators, our role is to explore other, perhaps more theoretical, aspects of travel and tourism, such as its impact on society and the environment. Tourism is a multidisciplinary subject which, as we have already seen, means that it encompasses a wide range of other perspectives.

However, the most common aspects that you will be asked to teach in schools and colleges will be occupationally related, preparing our learners to work in the industry.

Reflection 1.5

For each of the possible occupational environments listed in Figure 1.2, consider the range of knowledge and skills required to provide a service to the public.

Perhaps we can begin by considering the common ground. What skills and knowledge might be transferable from one sub-sector to another?

We have already suggested that there is an overlap and relationship between occupational sectors such as travel and tourism, retail and leisure. The basic business skills and knowledge of planning, marketing, customer service, and so on that are required to run our hypothetical hotel and an adventure holiday company or even a tour operations business, must be very similar. In fact, the structure of the Qualification Curriculum Framework (QCF), which we discuss in Chapter 2, reflects this in its credit framework and our learners very quickly become aware of the wider implications of their chosen career pathway.

The organization of the industry

With so many activities available under the umbrella of travel and tourism, is there an organizational framework to support and monitor them? How does central government influence, fund or regulate the industry? Surely, there does need to be some kind of central organization to coordinate the organizations supporting the travel and tourism industry. Our interest, of course, is in the bodies specifically responsible for education and training but it is important to understand how they relate to the overall organizational structure.

We have already noted how governments get involved in tourism either directly or indirectly through influencing or nurturing organizations that foster tourism. The direct intervention might be immigration control or licences for airlines to operate. However, indirectly, the funding of transportation route improvements which may be seen to provide primarily for the local population can also have a major impact on the tourism industry. Many of these activities come under the auspices of different government departments, rather than overtly within a department for tourism.

In the UK Government, the department responsible for tourism is the Department of Culture, Media and Sport (DCMS) whose aim is 'to improve the quality of life for all through cultural and sporting activities, to support the pursuit of excellence and to champion the tourism, creative and leisure industries' (DCMS website – see the Appendix at the end of this book). As we mentioned earlier, the DCMS has a policy document *Winning: A Tourism Strategy for 2012 and Beyond*, which draws on the 1999 strategy *Tomorrow's Tourism* (DCMS 1999). Ministers from the DCMS put in place a wide-ranging tourism reform programme in 2002, based on a strong relationship with 'partners in both public and private sectors', which is driven by improvements in delivery in key areas. The partners, Visit Britain, Regional Development Agencies, the Tourism Alliance and People 1st all play a role in developing tourism, its people or its infrastructure.

Visit Britain and its counterparts, Visit England, Visit Wales, Visit Scotland and Discover Northern Ireland, were established as strategic, marketing-focused bodies in April 2003. Within each national area, regional development agencies (RDAs), of which there are nine in England for example, now have strategic responsibility for tourism in their regions.

The Tourism Alliance was established in 2001 as a single voice for the tourism sector, with a remit to represent the sector's views and concerns more effectively to the government. Their impressive membership list includes a wide range of organizations involved in the industry and provides a comprehensive base for lobbying the government.

The Tourism Advisory Council, launched in April 2009, whose membership is drawn from industry, aims to provide a channel of direct regular contact between government and the industry.

Regional marketing organizations, known as destination marketing organizations (DMOs), have other responsibilities too, such as economic regeneration. The synergy between the regional strategies of regeneration and tourism are strong as many areas have placed their future firmly in the hands of tourism, for example Blackpool (http://www.reblackpool.com/). In Chapter 6 you will read that these organizations are great teaching resources.

There are many other organizations set up by governments to regulate particular elements of the travel and tourism industry. One such example is the UK Civil Aviation Authority (CAA), which:

- ensures that UK civil aviation standards are set and achieved
- regulates airlines, airports and National Air Traffic Services economic activities and encourages a diverse and competitive industry
- manages the UK's principal travel protection scheme, the Air Travel Organizers' Licence (ATOL) scheme, licenses UK airlines and manages consumer issues
- brings civil and military interests together to ensure that the airspace needs of all users are met as equitably as possible (http://www.caa.co.uk/default. aspx?catid=286, accessed 14 Feb. 2010).

The tourism industry could not function without other government departments such as the UK Border Agency and the UK Identity and Passport Service, for obvious reasons. Their policies and procedures provide great case studies for teaching.

There are too many other government departments and interventions at national and local levels involved in various aspects of the industry to mention in this text. Other authors provide more in-depth material and analysis than is possible in this publication. As educators for the travel and tourism industry, we will draw on expertise of People 1st, described earlier, who advise on the national strategy for the development of the people within the industry, including qualification development. One further organization that offers great support for the teaching of tourism is Springboard UK, an industry-based organization with a long history of working to promote careers in the industry, especially within the education environment, providing a free specialist careers information and advice service. In Chapter 6 you will be referred to their resources to assist in teaching.

Let us now consider industry organizations we need to be aware of for teaching purposes.

Knowing about industry organizations

As has been referred to earlier, the membership of the Tourism Alliance provides a comprehensive, but not exhaustive, list of some 50 interest groups related to the wider industry (see the Tourism Alliance website, in the Appendix). It would hard to pick from this list those organizations that have more importance or influence than others as each has its own area of expertise. However, some organizations are at the forefront of the industry, and curriculum considerations would expect our teaching to cover their role. Figure 1.3 lists just a few, which in our opinion, your teaching will touch on most often.

A particularly good source of industry information and case studies is Tourism Insights: 'a subscription service written by tourism professionals that monitors, analyses and interprets trends in the UK tourism market – essential reading for anyone serious about tourism' (http://www.insights.org.uk/).

- The Association of British Travel Agents (ABTA)
- Association of Independent Tour Operators
- British Transport Association
- Association of Leading Visitor Attractions
- British Hospitality Association
- Confederation of Passenger Transport UK
- Events Industry Alliance
- National Trust
- The Camping and Caravanning Club
- Tourism Society
- UKinbound

Figure 1.3 Selected members of the Tourism Alliance

Reflection 1.6

Consider planning an educational visit to Venice for your learners.

Make a spider gram of all the organizations that may affect the process of planning and organizing the visit and those who will ensure that it runs smoothly from the moment that you leave home until the moment that you step back onto home territory.

The People 1st sector skills council

Finally, but by no means least, we have already referred to People 1st on a number of occasions, which is an indication of the importance of their role. They are the sector skills council responsible for the training and development of people in not only the travel and tourism industry, but also hospitality and leisure. Clearly they are central to our work as teachers.

Teaching and learning for the travel and tourism industry

Knowledge of working practices and, indeed, an understanding of how people, both those who work within it and their clients, view it, must be a main driver for any vocational teaching and learning programmes. We shall be visiting some of these in Chapter 2, but to generalize, there are those that train people in the skills and knowledge we have considered above, and others that educate in the underpinning principles of the industry. However, the practice of teaching and learning does not take place in isolation. We have already seen that a vast number of stakeholders are involved in our sector, and education is constantly under scrutiny from the public in general and from the government.

What we teach and the way that we teach is undoubtedly influenced by these 'stakeholders'. Thus we will review policies and initiatives that have had an impact on the teaching of travel and tourism, on educational practices and on the nature of those who may be our learners.

Government policy and national initiatives

Undoubtedly, next to the learners, the Government, as the main funding body for education and training through the Department for Children, Schools and Families (DCSF), and the Department for Business Innovation and Skills (BIS), has to be a major stakeholder with an interest in developing knowledge, understanding and skills for the industry. Thus they will have the dominant influence in shaping the vocational curriculum largely through a range of policy statements and White Papers passed on to the educational community through Parliament.

The involvement of government in vocational education and training does, of course, date back at least to the beginning of the twentieth century. However, the origins of the current policies can be traced back to the 1980s and the beginnings of a

'New Vocationalism' arising out of a reaction against what was perceived as a failure of the liberal education of the 1950s and 1960s to prepare young people with the skills for employment. Consequently, the 1980s saw a plethora of initiatives designed to address what was seen as a shortfall in employable skills. It is not within the remit of this publication to examine these in detail, and more can be found in other publications such as *Teaching and Training in Post Compulsory Education* by Armitage et al. (2007). However, it is important to note that the new initiatives are not purely a phenomenon of the twenty-first century.

Yet even in the first ten years of the twenty-first century, there has been a whole raft of initiatives, reports and White Papers affecting the development of vocational education and training, all of which are important, but we will highlight those that seem to be immediately relevant to our cause.

Each of these initiatives has had considerable impact on the opportunities for learners (and thus the profiles of learning groups) and on the structure of the curriculum, so it is worth spending a few moments considering them.

Reflection 1.7

What do you know about the following?

- 14–19 Opportunity and Excellence
- Tomlinson Report: 14–19 curriculum and qualifications reform
- 14–19 Education and Skills White Paper
- Young Apprenticeships
- Modern Apprenticeships
- The Leitch Report
- Every Child (Learner) Matters
- Success for All.

14–19 Opportunity and Excellence (2003)

This policy document addressed the agenda for a more coherent programme for 14–19 learners and outlined many initiatives that would transform the provision of education for this phase. For our purposes the main ones were: providing opportunities for entry to employment, including: Modern Apprenticeships and pre-vocational programmes; the stimulation of collaboration between educational establishments and work-based training providers; providing financial support through the Educational Maintenance Allowance (EMA); offering a much stronger vocational programme with a firm underpinning of general education and developing a unified framework of qualifications suitable for all young people of all abilities.

The Tomlinson Report (2004)

It was as a result of this last proposal that a working group chaired by Mike Tomlinson was charged to advise the Government on the long-term 'shape of reforms'. The final report was published in October 2004 proposing sweeping changes to the whole education programme for the 14–19 phase that would indeed have provided a coherent, 'unified framework' of qualifications. Unfortunately, this appeared to be too drastic a solution and the eventual model which was based on the group's proposals focused largely on the vocational education elements and were reincarnated as the new 14–19 Diplomas, a mere shadow of Mike Tomlinson's vision.

14–19 Education and skills White Paper (2005)

Setting out the general agenda for the development of 14–19 education and skills, this White Paper addressed a number of issues from the modification of A/AS levels to the introduction of functional skills and the new 'specialized' diplomas, as we have seen above, modelled on the Tomlinson recommendations with significant input from employers through the relevant sector skills councils (see earlier). From the point of view of this publication, these two points are important since they will have an impact on how we teach our programmes of travel and tourism: functional skills are to be embedded into the curriculum and the pedagogical emphasis in vocational education programmes will, naturally enough, be on experiential and applied learning (www.literacytrust.org.uk/socialinclusion/youngpeople/1419paper).

Young Apprenticeships

Launched in September 2004, the Young Apprenticeships (YA) scheme enabled learners at Key Stage 4 in partnership with schools, colleges and employers to take vocational qualifications. They spend three days at school following their normal academic studies and two days on the YA programme. The teacher of travel and tourism may well be involved with these learners since apart from structured work experience, they take a level 2 qualification such as a National Diploma and a National Vocational Qualification (NVQ) level in travel services (www.skillsactive.com/training/apprenticeships/young-apprenticeships).

Modern Apprenticeships and Advanced Apprenticeships (2001)

Apprentices are full-time employees, doing a normal job 'building up knowledge and skills, gaining qualifications and earning money at the same time' and could be any age over 16. They will probably be working towards a work-based qualification such as an NVQ and may be operating in travel agencies taking bookings or advising clients, acting as resort reps or assisting at an airport check-in, for example. As a teacher, you might be responsible for managing the training and, particularly, assessing the development of these learners: in which case, you would need yourself to be qualified at NVQ level 3 assessor's award (A1 or A2) (www.apprenticeships.org.uk).

Leitch Report (2006)

Lord Sandy Leitch's report has at least stimulated much debate in the post-16 educational sector. Commissioned to review the state of the nation's skills needs, thought to be well below international standards, his recommendations placed responsibility for skills training largely in the hands of employers. Ninety-five per cent of adults are expected to achieve basic skills levels in functional literacy and numeracy, and 90 per cent should be qualified at least to level 2 in occupational skills. Additional funding is recommended to be routed through 'Train to Gain' schemes which provide funding for employers to provide training opportunities for their employees in collaboration with colleges and private training providers. Your adult learners will, quite possibly, be those released by employers under this scheme (www.dcsf.gov.uk/furthereducation).

Every Child (Learner) Matters (ECM)

We shall be reviewing the ECM agenda in Chapter 4 in the context of learning and teaching, but it is a government initiative that has had considerable impact on the way in which learning is managed in schools and colleges. Embedded in the Children Act (2004), its main purpose is to promote the development of each child or learner through the following principles:

- To be healthy.
- To stay safe.
- To enjoy and achieve.
- To make a positive contribution.
- To achieve economic well-being.

It is expected that every teacher plans to integrate these principles into every lesson where possible (Donovan 2005: 18–26).

The life experiences and aspirations of different groups of learners

Generalizations should come with a cautionary note: people are different and do not fit neatly into the categories we devise for them and, in any case, there is a danger that we might be led into stereotyping them and leading them, in turn, into the 'self-fulfilling prophecy' trap where they will behave in the manner expected of them according to the teacher's perceptions (Hargreaves et al. 1975).

Hyland and Merrill are clear that colleges of further education (FE) in particular are 'cosmopolitan institutions' that 'cater for everyone, 16–19 year olds, both academic and vocational, adult returners, access students, HE students, those with special needs, the socially excluded and those not involved anywhere else' (Green and Lucas 1999: 35, cited in Hyland and Merrill 2003: 47).

Schools too have now developed much broader curricula to include not only the traditional GCSE and A-level routes, but also applied learning programmes such as National Diplomas and the New (14–19) Diplomas.

Clearly, the 14+ lifelong learning sector must include a wide range of learners from young adults with perhaps inflated aspirations, to more mature students of travel and tourism who might be returning to work and/or study, seeking promotion through further professional development or perhaps a change in direction in their careers. What can we, as teachers, expect them to bring to the classroom and what do they expect from us? Here we try to identify their ambitions and needs so that we can create learning activities that will help them to achieve those aspirations.

Reflection 1.8

Case study (Figure 1.4): what advice would you give to Sarah in terms of pursuing a career in travel and tourism?

Sarah is a 19-year-old learner on the first year of a two-year BTEC Level 3 Travel and Tourism National Diploma.

It basically came down to two choices, I could stay at school and do A levels and go to university or I could go to the college and study on this course, and still go to university if I choose to. I guess I chose the course because I am really interested in it and do travel a lot with my family. Also it meant that I could study travel and tourism and not have to worry about taking A-level choices that I didn't really want to take. This way, I get to study stuff that interests me, I have no exams but still work really hard, and I get to enjoy the whole week. I am not sure exactly what I want to do at the end, I am hoping that my second year Work Based Experience unit will help me decide, but I don't feel any pressure to decide at this stage. My tutors are all people who have worked in travel and tourism in a number of exciting places, and I would like to do the kind of things that they have done.

Figure 1.4 Case study of a young travel and tourism learner

Aspirations of young adults

Our younger learners in this sector will be found largely in schools and in colleges of further education, although some may well be engaged in new apprenticeship programmes, and thus in full-time employment. We consider these programmes in detail in Chapter 2, so it should be sufficient at this stage to say that the programmes they will most likely be engaged in will be the New Diplomas, National Diplomas and Certificates, and NVQs.

Behavioural issues of the younger adult

So can we generalize about the characteristics and aspirations of these young people in a way that is helpful to developing programmes of learning that are meaningful to them, or are there differences for each learner that make such generalizations meaningless? Educationists, psychologists and sociologists have attempted to identify general characteristics of young learners which we perhaps ought to consider when designing our learning and teaching programmes.

From time to time, critics of the education system in the media, at governmental level, or even from within the educational community itself, have been critical of the education system in that it has been seen to be failing many young people. Donovan (2005: 9) points to Department for Education and Schools (DfES) statistics to support the view that there is a strong correlation 'between poor attendance and behaviour at school and later anti-social behaviour and criminality'.

Why are so many disaffected and 'failing'? Lumby and Foskett (2005: 77) point to a study of secondary school learners by Thomas et al. (2000) in which, '48 per cent found school always or sometimes boring, 21 per cent felt teachers never or hardly ever listened and . . . 25 per cent of 16-year-olds felt the worst thing about school was problems with particular lessons'.

Modern life does perhaps present our young learners (and indeed mature adults) with a whole set of bewildering problems, not least the very pace of life itself and the changes this brings. In 1976 Horrocks identified six 'points of reference' in viewing adolescence, but these still have validity today. It is a time when young people become more aware of an 'idealized self' and of physical development and 'body image'; a time of seeking status both as an individual and within a social group; and it is a time of intellectual expansion and evaluation of ideas (Horrocks 1976, cited in Harkin et al. 2001: 56).

Thus we are confronted by a range of emotions and ambitions in the travel and tourism classroom. The notion of the 'teenager' is a concept dating back to the 1940s (Savage 2008). It is a concept that has generated the creation of a youth culture which undoubtedly brings with it anticipated behaviours and expectations. So the abiding feature of the teenage years, and perhaps the most important aspect for us in planning a programme of learning, is the seeking out and establishing of an identity for the maturing adult: supporting the 'rite of passage' to an adult life of responsibility.

For our young adult who specifically wishes to study a programme of travel and tourism, this is their chosen route to a vocational identity: a place in the working environment of their social world, a world that is constantly and rapidly changing against a background of media and peer pressure and the ready availability of the vestiges of adult life such 'leisure drugs', alcohol and recreational sex.

The potential to motivate the younger learner

We have suggested above that one major contributory cause of lack of learner engagement and disaffection has been a lack of 'meaningfulness' of the subject and the manner in which it has been presented. Thus, extrapolating the foregoing argument, planning to teach vocational programmes such as travel and tourism offers the distinct possibility for developing environments that at least offer the possibility of 'meaningful learning' simply because they might be seen as being situated in the young learner's world of reality.

Given all these changes and developments, it is no wonder that young people in the classroom appear to behave in ways that will assert their individuality of body and mind. Chapter 4 proposes that there are ways to facilitate individual learning and to channel intellectual, social and emotional development to enhance learning.

At the same time, we should be wary of relying on a presumed interest in travel and tourism itself being enough to command engagement. We must also be aware that, for many, continuing education at 16 plus is merely a more attractive alternative to work and that a subject such as travel and tourism conjures up particularly attractive images. Of course, the Education and Skills Act 2008, based on the Green Paper, *Raising Expectations* (2007) will mean that all young people up to the age of 18 will soon compulsorily have to engage in some form of education and training, so developing the meaningful curriculum will become an even more urgent imperative.

Mature adults

Why, then, would a mature adult wish to study travel and tourism?

Reflection 1.9

Case study (Figure 1.5): what factors would you take into consideration when preparing a learning programme for Mary?

Bearing in mind our previous comments about making generalizations, we would, nevertheless, suggest that there are three main groups of mature learners to consider. The first is the group that, having completed programmes at level 3 (A levels, National Diplomas and, perhaps, NVQs), want to continue their studies in greater depth in higher education at a university or even at a college of further education. These will generally fall within the age group of 19 to 25 years old.

The second group consists of learners probably, but not necessarily, from about 23 years old onwards, who, having opted out of education post-16 to start work or perhaps through family commitments, now wish to return to their studies. Undoubtedly, a number of these will have come from the group of disaffected learners discussed above: learners who, as more mature adults, have developed an identity that they feel they can develop through a career in travel and tourism. They might be engaged in any of the programmes considered in Chapter 2 at any level, but most likely those from level 2 onwards.

Finally, there will be those learners already employed in the industry seeking to develop their skills and knowledge through a programme of continuing professional

---

Mary is a mother of two children who are both at secondary school in Years 10 and 11. Now they are more independent, and having travelled a lot as a family, she has decided that she would like to return to education to study travel and tourism with a view to starting a new career.

The local college has offered an Open College Network Access programme which involves units that cover a wide spectrum of the industry's activities but also an NVQ in travel and tourism services.

Her husband works for a local business and is more than willing to support her initiative.

Figure 1.5 Case study of an adult travel and tourism learner

development (CPD). This group might include people involved in other career paths who are looking for a change in direction (we did suggest some related careers earlier). Their focus will probably be on higher-level programmes with specific professional outcomes, such as the level 4 City and Guilds Higher Professional Diploma in Supervisory Management which will enable them to aspire to hotel management or travel agency management.

The particular profiles of these learners can be identified through their descriptions: some will have in-depth experience of the industry already, while others may have virtually none apart from days out or their annual holiday. However, almost certainly, they will all have one thing in common: because they have chosen to take this course of study, often against the odds and at personal cost, they will be highly motivated. Furthermore, most of them will have had experience of the world of work or at least of the rigours of adult life.

Generally, adults who have a wider experience of the world may have a clearer idea about the realities and will probably have made reasoned choices to seek qualifications that will enable them to work in the industry, change direction in their career paths or enhance their existing qualifications.

Clearly, all this has implications for the approach that we might take with mature adults, as opposed to how we might plan to teach younger students of travel and tourism who are either still a part of the compulsory education phase or within two or three years of this. We consider this in more detail in Chapter 4.

What of the future? The changing tourism industry

Over the past 20 years the travel and tourism industry has been affected by changes that previously could not have been imagined, or anticipated. The huge increase in personal computer ownership has affected the way people research and book holidays, while terrorist activities and national disasters have changed destination demand and air transport (overnight in some cases). The demographic of populations has also changed the holiday product. Changes provide interesting case studies through which the study of the development, impact and management of tourism can be carried out.

The changes could be categorized into social, technological and political, and all have an economic impact on the industry.

Social impacts include the changes in Western industrialized countries which have an ageing demographic. The older traveller is known to take more holidays, owing to higher disposable income, but they may also have different needs, in both the support they need while travelling, such as increased assistance owing to limited mobility, and the types of activities in which they want to participate at their destination. This has led to specialist tour operators such as SAGA, but also niche tourism such as food and wine, 'gourmet' tourism and 'achievement' tourism, such as walking the Machu Picchu trail.

At the other end of the generation market, it has become a trend for younger travellers to take a 'gap' year, which has encouraged tour operators and travel agents to specialize in long-haul travel, low-budget accommodation and volunteer-work packages. Destinations have also adapted by providing similar packages to dovetail to these tours, for example, the Australia tour bus 'Oz Experience', a hop-on-hop-off sightseeing bus around Australia's Eastern coast. Similar tours are also available for the higher-budget traveller.

The massive increase in cruise holidays seen since 2000 has changed this elite form of tourism in the twentieth century to the new mass tourism experience in the twenty-first century. Ships carrying thousands of passengers are common, bringing mass tourism to ports all over the world. There are many discussions to be had about this type of visitor and their benefit (or lack of benefit) to local economies, as the thousands of travellers spend a limited time in port, primarily eating and being entertained on the ship. The difference for a destination between being a 'port of call' or a port where both staff (and customers) join the ship can have a varying impact on the local economy. One may generate new accommodation opportunities and services for the support of the cruise industry, while the other may just receive day visitors, who take their meals and entertainment on the ship.

Reflection 1.10

List as many different demographic groupings as you can think of, and match different types of holiday and/or destinations unique to each group.

New outbound markets such as destinations in Australasia and Asia have chal- lenged traditional holiday destinations in Europe and the USA, who in response change their product to reclaim customers. This mirrors what happened in the 1960s and 1970s when European and USA destinations rivalled UK destinations. European destinations have changed with low-cost airlines, which have helped open the short- break market, and multiply the number of holidays people take. It is quite possible for UK residents to fly to a European destination for two days; a weekend break for dinner in Madrid or Nice is not beyond the price range of many people, nor beyond the effort of travelling, since it takes less time than travelling from Newcastle to London by car.

This increase in travel by the masses, particularly by air, brings with it much discussion about adding to the global warming crisis. European organizations such as Tourism Concern lobby to make international travel more responsible, while local communities lobby to keep airlines flying into their regional airports to help develop and support the tourism market at the destination. On the other hand, other groups campaign to reduce or prevent airport expansion.

The technological changes of the Internet have had a massive impact on the travel industry, while providing new and interesting forms of tourism in destinations such as Disney World, Florida. Booking a holiday has never been so easy for the individual; the process begins by researching destinations, formerly the domain of the travel agent. Guidance about destinations is readily available, while flights can be compared easily on the Internet. Organizations such as easyJet have expanded to link together all the components through easy-to-navigate websites. Similarly, airlines such as British Airways have had to review their working practices and charges, as the passengers move away from paying for premium services, especially on short-haul flights. These developments have challenged the high street travel shop; warnings abound for such companies, recommending them to specialize and offer a high quality service, for which people will pay a premium.

This is causing changes in employment. Many airlines no longer have their own ground staff but use handling companies to check in passengers and deal with luggage. Customers are asked to pay for what was once included in the price, such as food, sitting in a particular seat or viewing in-flight entertainment. Travel agency businesses looking for an edge in the marketplace are offering 'dynamic packaging', where a company will put together for the consumer a package taken from multiple suppliers, each offering the lowest price, rather than booking with one tour operator.

Reflection 1.11

Think about the airline industry and map out the range of businesses from budget airlines to premium airlines.

Or

Explore a low-cost airline website to see how many different services or components of the tourism industry can be booked through one website.

Terrorism has had a number of effects on travel since the turn of the century. After 9/11 the numbers of business travellers, particularly to America, dropped dramatically. There have been studies and texts written purely on this subject in recent years. Companies found alternative ways to do business, such as videoconferencing. Similarly, destinations that have had the misfortune to be targeted by terrorists, such as Bali and Egypt, have had to work hard to regain their visitor numbers. Tourists deserting these destinations have had a major and immediate economic impact on the local economy.

Security measures, introduced to limit the impact of terrorism, have caused changes in the way one travels through the airport, causing delays to passengers, expanding travelling time (on the ground rather than in flight). Tighter security has seen the introduction of 'bio passports' at an increased cost to the traveller, with new security measures such as body scanners being installed at airports, raising new issues.

The green lobby, referred to earlier, campaign for people to take responsibility for their travel through such programmes as 'offsetting' carbon emissions.

All these factors have an impact on the teaching of travel and tourism, challenging the teacher to keep abreast of developments, on the one hand, but making it a dynamic and ever-changing curriculum subject to engage the interests of our learners, on the other.

Summary

In this chapter we have attempted to present an overview of travel and tourism as a curriculum area. To many non-specialists it might appear to be a subject lacking in depth: we hope that this chapter has helped to allay those perceptions and give those dedicated to its promotion information to convince their doubters.

We have considered the contribution it makes to the nation as a whole in terms of the economy and to the development of society, but also its potential as an activity to give meaning to and to change people's lives. Clearly, the wide range of activities available in the sector creates opportunities to satisfy all types of individual needs and this, in turn, creates opportunities for careers. We have considered the range of skills, knowledge and understanding needed to service the industry, the organizations that provide opportunities for education and training, and government initiatives that have supported their activities. We have tried to analyse the nature of the learners we can expect to encounter in our classes and to introduce the reader to their teaching environment. Finally, we have brought the debate up to date by considering the ever-changing nature of travel and tourism and the challenges this poses for the teacher.

Our aim has been to provide a background to the learning and teaching environment which will inform the way in which we deliver our learning programmes in travel and tourism, which is the main object of this publication.

But what of the future of the educational scene? At the time of writing, major changes in the political scene are possible, and undoubtedly these will have implications for learning and teaching. We hope that this publication is sufficiently generic to be adaptable for any curriculum developments. Our next chapter looks at the context of curriculum development through the programmes in travel and tourism.

2

Programmes: developing the travel and tourism curriculum

In this chapter we will be looking at:

- the notion of 'curriculum'
- curriculum theory and practice in the context of travel and tourism programmes
- the national structure of qualifications in the UK
- the range of programmes and qualifications
- the teacher as a curriculum planner.

As a teacher of travel and tourism there are many different programmes on which you may be asked to teach. This chapter helps you understand the different qualifications, the different programmes, and their aims and purposes. We place the qualifications into the context of the National Qualifications Framework (NQF). We explain some of the different organizations involved in the delivery of education, in particular the awarding bodies. Later in the chapter we explore the syllabus and how to turn this document into a planned curriculum, and the purpose of schemes of work and how they relate both back to awarding bodies syllabus and forward to lesson plans.

Introduction: what is the curriculum?

'Programmes' of travel and tourism really provide us with the structure for our curriculum. But what do we mean by 'curriculum'? This chapter aims to unravel some of the mysteries of the notion and to examine the theory behind the many programmes that make up the travel and tourism curriculum.

Reflection 2.1

Think about your own most recent experience as a learner. What subject(s) were you studying?

What else did you learn while on this course?

What was your 'curriculum'? What do you think we mean by the 'curriculum'?

One key educationist was Lawrence Stenhouse, who, although writing in 1975, has had considerable impact on the development of our concepts of curriculum. He began by referring to the definition in the *Shorter Oxford English Dictionary*: 'a course: especially a regular course of study as at a school or university' (1975: 1). This is derived from the Latin which referred to running a course. In this case, curriculum might be described as 'the planned intentions of government and of teachers/trainers in their organisations' (Armitage et al. 2007: 180).

However, Stenhouse really considers that there is more to it than this. He points us to the 'reality of teaching and learning for teachers and students' (Armitage et al. 2007: 180). In other words, it is the totality of the learning experience which would include such factors as the general aims of the institution: is its primary aim to prepare people for university education or for an occupational role? Is there a focus on citizenship, preparing people for a 'useful' role in society? It would also include the teacher's priorities: do they see themselves as mere purveyors of knowledge, or do they want their learners to develop as autonomous learners who can organize their own learning? Although, as we shall see, these notions are not always obvious they undoubtedly do have an impact on the curriculum and, therefore, are often referred to as the 'hidden curriculum'. So, Stenhouse was arguing that the study of curriculum is important because we should 'examine [the] balance between intentions and realities and use this information to improve [our] work and enhance students' learning' (Armitage et al. 2007: 181).

Tony Nasta (1994: 21) helps us a little here when he makes a distinction between a 'course' and a 'programme'. In his view, a course 'reflects the traditional world of vocational education . . . The pedagogical model is paramount, namely that there is a recognised body of knowledge which has to be imparted'. However, a 'learning programme challenges all these conventions . . . It is the integration of knowledge and skills . . . [in which] learning becomes a partnership between the teacher as facilitator and the student' (ibid.). You will find that we generally talk about 'programmes' rather than 'courses' in this publication. This is because we believe that the curriculum is about the totality of the learning experience.

Reflection 2.2

Now reconsider the definition that you came up with in Reflection 2.1 in light of the above.

Think about a particular 'course' that you have undertaken at any time in your career and try to analyse what your teacher(s) were aiming to achieve in terms of your own development.

Has your perception of 'curriculum' changed at all? If so, in what way?

Behind all this discussion, then, there is a deeper meaning that can help us, perhaps, to understand the development of our travel and tourism programmes and why there are so many different types, and to compare and contrast them.

Curriculum ideologies and travel and tourism programmes

The most obvious starting point is to say that travel and tourism is a working industry and that people who want to be employed in it need to acquire certain specific skills. A programme that just trains people for these skills (programmes such as NVQs for example) is known as instrumentalist. This is a view that currently seems to dominate educational policy as we saw in Chapter 1 where we referred to the 'New Vocationalism', or the overwhelming desire to improve the nation's skill base.

But what of the knowledge and understanding that underpins and informs this practice? Surely the travel agent has to have a good knowledge of travel geography or a tourism officer would benefit from understanding the motivational psychology of his visitors or the events manager would provide a better service if she had some idea of the social needs of her community? Programmes that focus on knowledge and understanding would be called 'academic'. This is a view that is known as 'classical humanism' since its roots go back as far the ancient Greeks who believed that progress was determined by the growth of human knowledge, although it is true that this privilege tended to be limited to the ruling elite.

However, there are many educationists who would be very critical of both of these types of programme because they are very limited in how they address wider educational aims. How do they prepare people to become independent, autonomous learners who can take responsibility for their own learning, for example? Such educationists, influenced by theorists and philosophers such John Dewey (1859–1952) and Carl Rogers (1902–87), set about designing a different type of curriculum which is known as 'progressivist humanist'. This is because it is 'learner centred' and focusses not so much on the subject matter as developing the study skills of learners by encouraging them to think for themselves and to question assumptions about the subject of study, in our case travel and tourism. The teacher would then facilitate and guide their research to help them in their studies, thus enabling them to develop as 'autonomous learners', a theme that you will find repeated often throughout this publication.

These different 'ideologies', or beliefs about the purpose of education, lead to certain styles of teaching and types, or models, of curriculum. First, there is the 'product' model that focuses on the *outcomes* of the programme (what can the learner do as result of the experience?). Then there is the 'content' model, which focuses on *what* is learnt and, finally, the 'process' model, which focuses on *how* people learn.

There is not space in this publication to explore this fascinating world of ideologies and curriculum models further, but there is ample literature on it and a good starting point would be *Teaching and Training in Post-Compulsory Education* by Andy Armitage et al. (2007).

As implied earlier, this is important when studying the various curriculum alternatives in travel and tourism programmes since they serve different purposes and have different ideologies that drive them.

Reflection 2.3

From what you know about each of the following and from considering the above, which ideology would best describe these programmes? Why do think that?

National Diploma in travel and tourism
A level in travel and tourism
A National Vocational Qualification (NVQ) in travel services
ABTAC (The Association of British Travel Agents [ABTA] Travel Agency Certificate)

To help you, start by thinking about what their main purpose is. For example is it to gain a specific qualification so that your learners can be employed, for example, as a children's representative with a tour operator? Or, will it give them Universities and Colleges Admissions Service (UCAS) points so that they can go to university?

You will probably have realized that most programmes have elements of some, if not all, of these ideologies and models. So how does this help us understand the pedagogy of our subject? That is, how do we teach travel and tourism or facilitate its learning?

The manner of our teaching/facilitating will be influenced by the type of programme, the content of the curriculum, our students' preferred learning styles and, indeed, by our own beliefs (or ideology) about education. For example, if we believe that the learners just need to know how to book a holiday using a specific information technology (IT) package, then our lessons may just consist of learning how to use it accurately, almost mechanically. On the other hand, if we want our learners to consider the physical, psychological and social impact of tourism on individuals, then we might lecture them on these factors and then set research projects for them to study one or two in some depth independently.

In order to develop our understanding of how we ought to promote learning on these programmes, it will be useful to know what they are and what they aim to provide for our learners.

The origins of travel and tourism programmes

We have already noted how, in the UK, the travel and tourism programmes first appeared as a distinct subject in higher education (HE) in the 1960s, though as Airey (2005) noted there are earlier examples of the serious study of tourism issues dating back to 1891. Tourism appeared as a module within other degrees, such as business studies, throughout this time and remains a contributing subject to many higher education programmes, such as geography, business, even urban planning. The growth of tourism programmes throughout the late twentieth century mirrored the growth of the industry and, combined with the professionalization of the tourism supplier, led many HE institutions to develop tourism programmes. The first distinct Master's-level programmes started in Surrey and Strathclyde universities in 1972. At the lower level, Travel and Tourism Higher National Diplomas (HNDs) were first offered in the late 1960s. Since this time, the number of programmes has grown, with universities and further education establishments seeing a demand from industry and responding with dedicated programmes. The content of programmes and their relationship to the vocational ideologies are discussed in depth by Airey and Tribe (2005). However, the latest addition to the range of travel and tourism programmes in HE has been the highly vocational Foundation Degrees. The introduction to the UK of Foundation Degrees in Arts (FDA) began in 2000 (DfEE 2000). The ethos is a clear vocational focus, to be achieved through transparent employer involvement in design and implementation. Foundation Degrees in Arts are to be 'academically rigorous' and 'vocationally relevant' (DfES Standards Unit 2004: 5). The validation of any FDA is expected to be based upon employers' needs and provide an employment-focused curriculum (DfEE 2000).

> Foundation Degrees should appeal to people who might otherwise not have considered entering higher education – people who have left schools and gone straight to work – as well as people who simply want a shorter qualification which will move them on quickly in their career in preference to the longer honours degree programmes.
>
> (DfEE 2000: 12)

The developments have continued to be endorsed through government reports such as the Leitch Report (DfEE 2006) as discussed earlier, which expanded the policy for greater employer involvement in all levels of education. The FE sector was deemed the best environment in which to deliver the FDA, with many programmes being delivered in a way that accommodates those in employment, either through distance packages or limited attendance at classes. Much of the assessment is based on employment situations. The expertise of FE sector staff in delivering to industry provides vocational understanding, while academic status comes from the involvement of universities.

Teaching of travel and tourism aimed at the 16–19-year-olds in the FE sector began with the introduction of National Diplomas in Leisure and Tourism in the 1980s, but continued through the 1990s to the present day, although the curriculum is now separated into two discrete awards, Travel and Tourism, and Sport. The most recent programmes to enter the scene crossing the FE and the compulsory schools sectors, are the 14–19 Diplomas. However, it was the FE sector which was the focus of many developments in the 1980s through to Curriculum 2000. The Business and Technology Education Council validated programmes for industry establishing the National Diplomas in Travel and Tourism as a leading programme, studied by many and respected by industry. The National Diploma (and its part-time equivalent the National Certificate) offered an alternative route to A levels, which at that time were only available in traditional curriculum subjects.

Qualifications with a vocational focus were a mid-way route between the purely academic A level and the strictly vocational qualifications such as Air Fares and Ticketing, ABTAC (ABTA Travel Agency Certificate). The BTEC Nationals were promoted by educationists desirous of seeing the subject developed and studied in depth, while the strictly vocational qualifications were spawned by the burgeoning instrumentalist ideology that we mentioned earlier. In the 1990s, the instrumentalist agenda was represented by NVQs and the academic by the newly introduced General National Vocational Qualifications which were aimed at replacing National Diplomas. As we have seen, instrumentalism tends to lead to a 'product'-driven curriculum: at the end of the programme the learners would have the skills to make them employable in the industry. The first of the GNVQs was piloted in FE in 1993. These dual-level qualifications (intermediate and advanced) offered alternatives to GCSE and A level. This period in the FE sector is acknowledged as leading in creativity and innovation in teaching practices (Donovan 2005; Hodgson and Spours 2003). This is important to this story because the qualifications were developing a different philosophy to the delivery and assessment of their qualifications. This was a more 'process'-driven curriculum, focusing on the development of study skills, learning how to learn, through research assignment activities.

Clearly, such different ideologies have implications for the pedagogy (how we teach) of our subject. Morrison and Ridley (1989) provide a very clear model (Figure 2.1) which, in summary, identifies how the ideology will influence the manner of delivery, the relationship between the teacher and learner, the way in which the programme will be assessed and the types of resources used. The latter two are discussed in Chapters 5 and 6 respectively, but you might like to consider how this might be applied in Reflection 2.4.

Until the Travel and Tourism GCSE was introduced in 2002, young people up to the age of 16 may have studied tourism as part of other subjects such as geography or in alternative programme to GCSEs, such as GNVQ Leisure and Tourism. The

	Progressivism/ learner-centred	Classical humanism/ academic	Instrumentalism
Emphasis	The individual learner	The acquisition of knowledge	The acquisition of skill
Theory of knowledge	Emphasis on the process of learning	Development of subject disciplines	Development of 'useful' knowledge and skills
Theory of learning and the learner's role	Experiential learning: development of learner autonomy	Obedience, passivity – accepting the teacher as the font of knowledge	Induction into vocationally relevant areas
Theory of teaching and the teacher's role	The teacher as facilitator of learning – guiding the learner towards autonomy	Instructor, information transmitter, authoritative formal tutor	Instructor, trainer transmitter of vocationally relevant experience
Assessment	Diagnostic, multiple criteria, informal profiling – fulfilling learner potential	Written, formal, attainment testing, examinations	Formal, written and oral (for example, key skills), practical
Resources	First-hand (from experience) and diverse	Second-hand (from textbooks and so on) and restricted	Narrowly relevant to the content, practical vocational.

Figure 2.1 How ideologies can influence the way in which a curriculum is delivered (adapted from Morrison and Ridley 1989: 50)

introduction of the GCSE qualification offered parity of esteem with other more traditional GCSE subjects. However, the latest developments are the *new* National Diplomas in Travel and Tourism being introduced in 2010. This will give travel and tourism a stronger presence in the curriculum. If you wish to explore the development of the vocational curriculum two further sources are Donovan (2005) and Hodgson and Spours (2003).

Reflection 2.4

With reference to Figure 2.1, which summarizes Morrison and Ridley's notion of 'pedagogical theories', complete the chart in Figure 2.2 for teaching each of the following:

(a) The impact of tourism on destinations.
(b) How to process a passenger's flight details.
(c) How to research and analyse the cultural mix of visitors in a locality.

We might hope that you will have identified the largely 'classical humanist' nature of (a) which asks the learners to engage in cognitive activity; the instrumentalist philosophy of (b) which focuses on practical application; and the humanist approach in (c) where the learners are engaging in process-based skills that will develop them as autonomous learners.

However, you may disagree with our analysis and might have found this exercise difficult because each example is perhaps ambiguous. In fact, what we generally find is that our curricula rarely fall totally within one particular school of thought, or ideology. More often than not there are aspects of each present and identification is more a question of emphasis where one ideology dominates. For example, all our

With reference to Reflection 2.3 and Figure 2.1, try to complete the following chart.

	The impact of tourism on destinations	How to process a passenger's flight details	How to research and analyse the cultural mix of visitors in a locality
Main focus – the learner, content or outcomes?			
What knowledge is developed? Process, product or subject matter?			
What is the learner's role?			
What is the teacher's role?			
How is it assessed?			
What resources are required?			

Figure 2.2 Interpreting Morrison and Ridley's theory

programmes will have objectives or some kind outcome in mind, even if this relates to the processes of learning rather than the development of a specific skill or knowledge set, so, arguably, there is always a 'product' in mind.

Bearing this in mind, then, we shall consider the range of programmes that you might encounter in schools and colleges today and you might like to reflect on the underpinning ideologies of each.

Range of programmes and qualifications

Levels and the NQF

To understand the context of these programmes you will need to also understand the overarching structure of the qualifications framework. The body responsible for accrediting all programmes that would be eligible for government funding is the Qualifications and Curriculum Development Agency (QCDA), the organization appointed by government to coordinate and validate all qualifications that fall within the National Qualifications Credit Framework (NQCF) and to oversee their examination.

It is their responsibility to review and monitor all qualifications offered by awarding bodies and to demonstrate how they fit into the framework: generally, programmes outside this will not be able to draw government funding. Currently, the framework is undergoing a major modification, changing from a National Qualification Framework (NQF) to a National Qualifications and Credit Framework (NQCF) to be launched in September 2010. The implication is that, in future, it will be possible for learners to gain credits from a variety of learning programmes, further enabling them to design their own programmes but, for our purposes, to help understand the concept of levels, in Figure 2.3 we illustrate some qualifications as they appeared in the NQF.

> **Reflection 2.5**
>
> Case study:
> Under the new credit system, a training provider can mix and match qualifications provided that the majority of the credits are achieved from an existing stand-alone qualification.
>
> Bethany studies on a BTEC level 3 Diploma in Travel and Tourism that incorporates an ABTAC qualification and a level 1 Airfares and Ticketing course.
>
> She will accumulate credits for each of these: what are the advantages for her in developing a career path? What is the range of environments in which she might be employable?

Under the new QCF, qualifications are made up of units that allocate credits as opposed to guided learning hours, and qualifications will be sized in terms of the number of credits that they generate.

Levels	Qualifications	
Level 4	HND	Foundation Degree
Level 3	National Diploma	A levels
Level 2	First Diploma	GCSE (a–c)
Level 1	Foundation Diploma	GCSE (d–g)

Figure 2.3 The National Qualifications Framework (adapted)

Introducing the programmes

GCSE (General Certificate of Secondary Education)

In England, GCSEs are graded A* to G, which is level 2, and D to G which is level 1 in the qualifications framework. GCSE qualifications are generally, but not always, taken as a two-year course by students aged 14 to 16 (Years 10 and 11). This is the most common qualification in England with over half a million young people sitting these examinations in 45 subjects each year, normally, but not exclusively, at age 16. It is the qualification by which the majority of the UK population record their educational achievement at the end of compulsory education. This qualification benchmarks young people against each other providing a comparative guide for both educationalists and employers to use for further education and/or job entry.

In England the National Curriculum dictates a core of GCSE subjects that must be studied to this level (Figure 2.4). It is a major indicator for ranking each

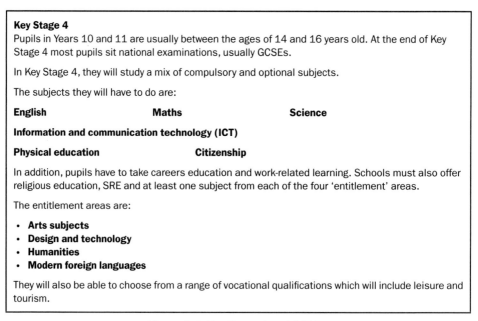

Key Stage 4

Pupils in Years 10 and 11 are usually between the ages of 14 and 16 years old. At the end of Key Stage 4 most pupils sit national examinations, usually GCSEs.

In Key Stage 4, they will study a mix of compulsory and optional subjects.

The subjects they will have to do are:

English   **Maths**   **Science**

Information and communication technology (ICT)

Physical education   **Citizenship**

In addition, pupils have to take careers education and work-related learning. Schools must also offer religious education, SRE and at least one subject from each of the four 'entitlement' areas.

The entitlement areas are:

- **Arts subjects**
- **Design and technology**
- **Humanities**
- **Modern foreign languages**

They will also be able to choose from a range of vocational qualifications which will include leisure and tourism.

Figure 2.4 Key Stage 4 and GCSEs

school's achievement. You will have noticed that travel and tourism is not a part of the core National Curriculum, it comes into the humanities group in the 'entitlement' areas. This means that the numbers of pupils, in state education, studying travel and tourism in any one school may change each year depending on the subjects offered at transition Key Stage 4.

AS and A level
AS and A level Travel and Tourism are level 3 qualifications that offer the opportunity for learners to study the subject in greater depth. Although there is a 'classical humanist', knowledge-based agenda here which is assessed in the appropriate manner by written examination, there is also a strong element of applied studies in which learners monitor and analyse tourism development, developing a deeper understanding of the impact of travel and tourism through learner-centred study of the more progressive humanist kind.

National Diplomas and Certificates
National Diplomas in Travel and Tourism are now offered at levels 2 and 3 by the Edexcel and OCR examination boards, whose roles we discuss in Chapter 5. However, as we have seen, they have their origins in the BTEC diplomas of the 1980s and developed a very distinct characteristic of their own as a process-driven, learner-centred programme with a focus on work-related learning. The popularity of these programmes among teachers (and industry), particularly in colleges of further education, is such that they have survived many threats to their existence, notably the introduction of the GNVQ qualifications in the 1990s, so that they are now firmly embedded in the qualifications framework. Although they include assignments that are externally set and examined, most assignments are set and assessed by the teachers who deliver the programmes, thus allowing some measure of autonomy and the possibility of structuring them to fulfil their own learners' needs, which might be related, for example, to the opportunities presented by the local environment. As we shall see in Chapter 5, standards are maintained through the application of rigorous external moderation.

The New Diplomas
The New Diplomas are the outcome of the Tomlinson Report of 2004 (Working Group on 14–19 Reform 2004) on the future of post-14 education in the UK, although, as we noted in Chapter 1, they are really but a shadow of his vision. As with others before him, Mike Tomlinson and his team were charged with suggesting ways in which all young learners from 14 to 19 years old might become better engaged with an education system that promoted equity between academic and vocational programmes. They concluded that the only way was to completely change the structure of the system and proposed a 'unified system of diplomas' which would mean replacing A levels and GCSEs.

> It is our view that the status quo is not an option. Nor do we believe further piecemeal changes are desirable . . .

> Our report sets out a clear vision for a unified framework of 14–19 curriculum and qualifications.
>
> (Working Group on 14–19 Reform 2004: 1)

Unfortunately, established views are perhaps too deeply entrenched for such radical change, so we are left with a model that is somewhat less than that envisaged.

Figure 2.5 presents a summary of the structure of the diplomas as they available now. In principle, they offer a holistic curriculum for every learner and to an extent do enshrine the Tomlinson view of a diploma that included not only elements of vocational education, but also prepared learners for a role in the wider world through a programme of 'generic learning'. This includes the development of functional skills, which would contextualize maths, English and ICT into their life worlds, and personal learning and thinking skills, which would prepare them for a more fulfilling role in society in general and in the workplace in particular. Chapter 3 deals with these matters in greater depth.

Again, the specifications are available on examination boards' websites, but you will see that they have followed a similar structure to that of the National and First Diplomas. Furthermore, there is also a substantial element of 'personalized and additional learning' which is intended to give the learner scope to follow other interests of their own and perhaps gain additional qualifications such as A levels, First or National Diplomas or even those that will prepare them to actually start a job of work in their chosen field, including NVQs or travel industry awards.

The requirements at each level are graded so that the learner will progress through a structured programme. Figure 2.6 illustrates the progressive cognitive skills at each level.

Higher National Diplomas and Certificates (HNDs/HNCs) and Foundation Degrees

It may be that you will find yourself teaching in a college that is accredited to teach programmes at higher education levels, in which case, you may teach on an HND or Foundation Degree in Travel and Tourism or Leisure and Tourism, which we discussed in some depth earlier. Learners on level 3 programmes such as National Diploma or A levels can find a natural progression to higher education. Again, the focus is generally work related and the curriculum model is process based, but the

Principle learning	Generic learning	Additional and/or specialist learning
Mandatory units	Functional skills:	Complementary learning, adding breadth or depth
The number varies according to the level and the learning line	English, maths, ICT	
	Personal, learning and thinking skills	Progression pathways
Sector-related		Choice
50% applied learning	Work experience (min. 10 days) project	

Figure 2.5 Structure of the New Diplomas

Foundation/level 1 – will provide a broad understanding of the travel and tourism industries, an appreciation of the centrality of customer service to the sector and an introduction to the financial and environmental aspects of travel and tourism.

Higher/level 2 – will provide an opportunity to develop the knowledge and understanding of the nature, extent and role of the travel and tourism sector, and those who work within it, the diversity of the sector, and the importance of finance and legislation in the sector.

Advanced/level 3 – will provide opportunities to analyse, evaluate and explore principles and practice relating to the travel and tourism sector in business, planning and management; legislation, development and sustainability; sales and marketing; customer service and career opportunities in the travel and tourism sector.

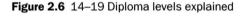

Figure 2.6 14–19 Diploma levels explained

level of study is at level 4 on the qualifications framework (HE level 1) with opportunities to progress to level 5 (HE level 2) modules and, further, even to top-up to an honours degree after another year's study.

In the spirit of extending the curriculum to challenge all learners, at the time of writing there have even been enquiries from schools with a view to developing an HND/C programme. So if your teaching environment is in schools, there may well be opportunities for you to extend your portfolio to begin teaching at HE levels.

National Vocational Qualifications: the instrumentalist agenda manifest
In Chapter 1, we noted the development of the New Vocationalism in the 1980s, with an agenda to improve the nation's skills base in order to become more competitive in the global economy, and the role of NVQs as a part of that agenda. One of the objects of the NVQ was to provide a unified, more coherent system of vocational qualifications. Whether this has been the case or not is open to debate and you must make up your own mind based on the evidence of your experience. However, NVQs are currently the system in use and you will most likely come across groups and individuals who are engaged in developing portfolios of evidence to achieve their qualification.

In terms of our ideologies and models, they most definitely would be seen to be instrumentalist and product based since they set out to ensure that the learners develop and provide evidence for the skills, knowledge and understanding to prove that they are competent in a specific job role such as an NVQ in Aviation Operations or an NVQ in Travel and Tourism Services. Specialist vocational qualifications in travel and tourism have been developed with professional bodies such as ABTA or the Institute of Leadership and Management (ILM).

The debate on 'competency-based assessment' (for that is what this is rather than learning) is prolific and it is worth spending a little time reading the varying points of view as in Hyland (1994), Wolf (2000) and Lea et al. (2003).

Nevertheless, many of our readers will either be working with groups that are developing their vocational skills through various awards or may even have their appetite whetted enough by this discussion to add an NVQ or similar award to their own curriculum as a means of providing a qualification for their learners that is accepted by the industry as a sign of competence in the workplace. Bethany in Reflection 2.5 is a case in point. They could, indeed, complement other programmes such as National Diplomas or as additional specialist learning in the New Diplomas, or could even be stand-alone programmes.

The National Open College Network (NOCN)

One of the most potent forces for change in adult education has been the development of the NOCN (Figure 2.7). Yet, as the National Institute of Adult Continuing Education (NIACE) observe in their document celebrating 25 years of the movement, it is one of the most closely guarded secrets in the history of education. Originally working mainly with adult returners, historically, it has been at the cutting edge of the credit-based framework and its programmes are validated by the QCDA and therefore have currency within the qualifications system and can draw down funding.

In principle, NOCN programmes are designed by teachers for their specific groups of learners, and thus are, perhaps, the most learner-centred programmes of all. Teachers can write their own units which are rigorously scrutinized by regional panels. We can personally vouch for the rigour from experience both as a programme reviewer and as having been reviewed! Approved modules then enter the national database and may be drawn down to be used to construct a personalized learning programme for specific groups of learners. NOCN units in travel and tourism include Careers in Leisure and Tourism; The Impact of Leisure and Tourism in the Environment; and The Use of Technology in Travel and Tourism.

Introducing the scheme of work

In this section we consider the importance of having a scheme of work and how to write one. First, let us look at what we mean by a scheme of work.

What is a scheme of work?

Up to this point, we have tried to draw your attention to the wider notion of the curriculum and how this affects the way in which we deliver our programmes of

---

NOCN Mission:
'The Open College Network supports learning and widens opportunity by recognising achievement through credit-based courses and qualifications.'

NOCN Values Statement:
- A belief in the entitlement of people to gain recognition for their achievements in learning and to fulfil their potential.
- Respect for and encouragement of diversity in learners and learning approaches, partners and settings.
- A passion to make a difference to disadvantaged individuals, groups and communities.
- An ambition to open up opportunities for vocational progression and personal and social development.
- A commitment to integrity and ethical business practices.

Figure 2.7 NOCN mission and values statement (www.nocn.org.uk/about-us/mission%2c-vision-and-values accessed 30 Jan. 2010)

learning. The scheme of work might be considered to be the document that is the manifestation of that curriculum. It is the mid-, to long-term strategic plan in which you define your beliefs by the aims and objectives and by the ways in which you intend to structure learning, teaching and assessment. Do we want our learners to develop as independent, autonomous learners, or are we content if they just do enough to complete an assignment or pass an examination? This would lead us to a discussion about 'deep and surface learning', but is a topic for Chapter 4.

At this point you might like to refer back to Figure 2.1, the Morrison and Ridley model, for analysis of the curriculum.

Reflection 2.6

Referring to Figure 2.1 and in light of your reading so far, what are your preferred approaches to teaching, learning and assessment now?

Have they changed at all?

How would this affect the way in which you might design a scheme of work?

As the mid-, to long-term plan for a programme of learning, the scheme of work sets out the way in which we intend to achieve the specific learning outcomes of the course in question as defined by those who design it, generally the awarding body, but it could be you, the teacher, in the case of an NOCN programme, for example.

Why do we need a scheme of work?

In the past, students on initial teacher training programmes often returned from their placements with tales of schemes of work that were written on the back of an envelope or their mentors would claim that they were 'in their head'. In these days of greater accountability to senior management and ultimately to Ofsted, this is less frequently, if ever the case. Many institutions have their own template for a scheme of work, and lesson plans, in order to present a corporate policy towards the planning of learning: this in itself might be seen as a statement of the institution's 'hidden curriculum'. So, why is the scheme of work seen as such an important feature?

Reflection 2.7

The importance of this mid- to long-term planning might seem to be obvious. We hope it is, but it is worth spending a few moments considering this.

List all the reasons that you can think of to justify the need for a scheme of work.

We hope that you came up with some of the following and maybe more:

- It is a way of organizing the content of a programme in a logical order to ensure learner development of knowledge, understanding and skills.
- It enables us to plan strategies that are appropriate to specific topics in a way that will enhance learning.
- It is a guide to lesson planning.
- It will enable us to plan when and how we will assess learning either through formative or summative procedures. (We will visit this in Chapter 5.)
- It enables us to plan ahead for special resources that might need to be booked such as a computer suite, fitness testing equipment, visiting speakers or visits to external venues. (Chapter 6 deals with this.)
- It will help your colleagues or line manager to integrate your scheme of work into the planning for the wider curriculum and enable somebody else to teach your lesson should you be absent.
- Tight planning of a scheme of work will, paradoxically, enable you to be more flexible, taking into account any unforeseen events or even adjusting to the needs of learners who advance more quickly than you had anticipated.

So, with all this in mind, we should ask the question, how should we go about designing a scheme of work and what should be in it?

Figure 2.8 presents a diagrammatic view of the process: starting with the basic premise of the programme specifications, the learning environment and your expertise as a teacher of leisure and tourism, your plan should reflect the needs of your learners and organize the experience to inform the individual lesson plan.

Designing the scheme of work

Reflection 2.8

Thinking about the issues discussed above, make a list of what you think should be in a comprehensive scheme of work and justify your selection.

What should be in the scheme of work?

As we have said, many institutions will have their own templates and, generally, they will include the following (as should your answer to Reflection 2.8) and maybe more:

- **General information:** it is, first, worth making a note of the various factors that may affect our planning – how many weeks are there to complete the programme? How long is each session? And, if we are to plan programmes appropriate to learners' needs – how many students are there in the group? What is the

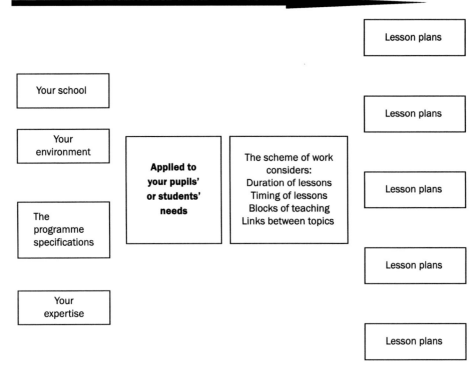

Figure 2.8 Diagrammatic view of the scheme of work planning process

group profile? What is their experience of the subject to date? Are there any students who might need special attention?

- **The aims, general objectives and learning outcomes:** these will be informed by the awarding body's specifications but will need to be organized in a logical order for our teaching purposes.

- **Content:** again this is where you will order the sequence of learning activities, probably informed by the aims, objectives and learning outcomes and taking into account such activities as assessments and planned visits.

- **Teaching and learning methods:** planning at this stage will ensure that you consider the most appropriate methods for each topic and plan for variety.

- **Assessment methods and timing:** this will, again, enable you to consider the most appropriate and valid methods for each topic or for the course overall (whether assignments, role play, presentations, examinations or tests) and the timings.

(based on Petty 2004: 441–2)

The teacher as curriculum planner

Given all this information, where then do we start with our design?

Reflection 2.9

Figure 2.9 is part of the specification from the BTEC National Diploma Travel and Tourism with the learning outcomes.

- If you were aiming to teach this module over a period of six three-hour sessions, what would be the best order to teach each topic?
- Why would you do it this way?
- If you are unfamiliar with this topic, please choose another from any set of specifications.

---

1. Know the components of Travel and Tourism and how they interrelate
Components of travel and tourism: accommodation; transport; tour operations; tourist development and promotion
Interrelate: chains of distribution; integration; interdependencies
Types of tourism: domestic; inbound; outbound

2. Know the roles and responsibilities of travel and tourism organizations within the different sectors
Roles and responsibilities: to meet main organizational aims; to provide services and products
Sectors: profit sector; no-for-profit sector

3. Understand how recent developments have shaped the present day travel and tourism industry
Recent developments: from the 1960s to the present day
Present day travel and tourism industry: such as products and services and contribution to GDP

4. Understand the trends and factors affecting the development of travel and tourism
Trends: increased frequency of holidays, flexibility of booking, and so on
Factors: natural disasters, health warnings, terrorism, and so on
Development: such as new products and services

Figure 2.9 Unit content from Edexcel Level 3 BTEC Nationals in Travel and Tourism: Investigating Travel and Tourism

'There is too much information on a topic' (PGCE Leisure and Tourism trainee teacher 2007). This is a quote from a PGCE student, who expressed a concern common among new teachers, 'How can I fit it all in?' This experience is recognized by Petty (2006) adding his own comments:

> Many teachers know far more than they can hope to explain in the time they are allowed.
>
> . . . if content is delivered too fast the working memory and short-term memory soon get swamped
>
> . . . students [learners] need time to familiarise themselves with new content.
>
> (Petty 2006: 26–7)

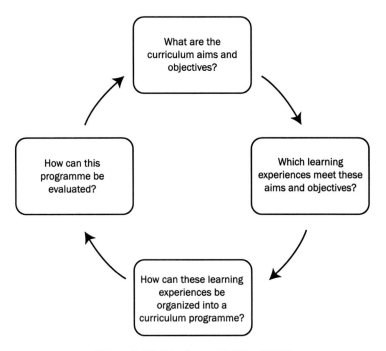

Figure 2.10 Tyler's model (Tyler 1971)

The means by which we ensure that teaching delivers the outcomes intended is to undertake careful planning which provides a structure through which the individual teacher can plan and deliver to an individual class.

One model for designing the curriculum that has been useful for a number of decades is Ralph Tyler's very simple model (1971). Figure 2.10 illustrates this. You will notice that the first premise is that the designer will need to know exactly what the aims, objectives and learning outcomes should be. In a way, this would suggest a 'behaviourist', product approach to the curriculum and this has drawn much criticism, particularly from progressive humanists who favour the process curriculum. However, as we have noted elsewhere, arguably, if the process of learning is a desired result of the learning programme it might still be described as an 'outcome'.

Reflection 2.10

Using Tyler's model, sketch out a curriculum for one (or more) of the following:

- How to conduct a welcome session for a tour party
- How to research the travel needs for a particular demographic group such as the over-50s
- How to organize and book an educational visit for a group of young people

Using Tyler's model, we need to define what it is we would like our learners to achieve, our outcomes, since this gives us purpose and direction. Unless we are writing our own programme, as we might with NOCN, then generally the guidance we need might be found in the awarding bodies' specifications.

The teacher's role, as a curriculum planner, is to take the syllabus from the awarding body and plan a programme of learning that suits a particular group of pupils or students, utilizing industry experience and local resources – human, physical and environmental. Chapter 6 explores some resources available to teach travel and tourism. No matter what the level or programme, every teacher has to go through a process of taking the syllabus outline and developing a scheme of work leading to effective individual lessons. It may seem like a great deal of work to plan for the year ahead, but the detail added in the early stages will pay off later in time saved and a secure feeling that you are in control of the learning (and your workload).

The planning process

This process has to begin with the syllabus from the awarding examination body. This document will give you guidance as to the number of learning hours in which you will be expected to deliver the programme of study; how the unit links to transferable skills and additional learning for citizenship and enterprise that may be incorporated; and, most importantly, the *learning outcomes* expected from your learners. Your scheme of work should also take into account the form of assessment: you may have to accommodate practice test/examinations or time for portfolio building into the scheme of work.

Your planning should also take into account your school or college environment, plus the time of year that you are delivering the programme. Are there any days where other activities may impact on your teaching plan, such as open days, sports days or pupil review days? Are you going to lose some teaching time because of bank holidays? Your plan may also consider the time of day, and the day in the teaching week of your delivery of the lessons. This may influence the kind of activities that you engage your learners in: for example, students react differently after a PE lesson or the first lesson on Monday morning or the last on Friday afternoon. With thoughtful consideration of such things, an imaginative teacher plans to overcome the ebbs and flows in learners' mood changes. Once you have confirmed the length, number of hours and time slots of your planned teaching, you can begin to deconstruct the programme specifications and reconstruct them into a scheme of work for your particular circumstances, building up learning in a sequential manner. Remember the syllabus will not have been written in a format that can be directly transposed into a scheme of work. It is your expertise that sees the links between topics, your learners and your environment. See Figure 2.11 for an exemplar scheme of work.

The topics taken from the syllabus should be placed into logical progressive steps to take your pupils' or students' through to the learning outcomes required for success. In one sense you have to work backwards from the learning outcomes, planning individual sessions that build into a scheme of work. Competency outcomes are common and drawing on Bloom's taxonomy (see Figure 4.3, page 72), which we visit

Course objectives At the end of the course, the learner will be able to:
1. Know the roles and responsibilities of different categories of holiday representatives.
2. Understand the legal responsibilities of a holiday representative.
3. Understand the importance of health and safety in relation to the role of the holiday representative.
4. Be able to apply social, customer service and selling skills when dealing with transfers, welcome meetings and other situations.

Session L/O	Topic/aim	Tutor activity	Learner activity	Assessment of learning	ECM	Resources
w/c 25 Jan **Lesson (a)** L/O 1	Introduction to unit and assessments	Introduce, go through assignments, outline activity, support & feedback	Discuss assignments, prepare role plays	Displayed understanding upon questioning	2, 3, 4 **C3.1a** **PS3.1**	SOW, role play scenarios
w/c 25 Jan **Lesson (b)** L/O 1	Overseas representative/ customer service agent	Direct small group research of job descriptions from a selection of companies Ppt presentations	Questioning, discussion Contrasting content Note-taking, presentations	Displayed understanding upon questioning	2, 3, 4 **C3.1b** **ICT3.1**	IT access for research tasks
w/c 01 Feb **Lesson (a)** L/O 1	The typical day and week of a holiday representative	Outline of main role and duties, set research task, provide guidance and feedback	Discussion of different duties, using descriptions to prepare poster presentations	Questions and answers, discussion and feedback on guides	2, 3, 4	Computer terminals in LRC
w/c 01 Feb **Lesson (b)** L/O 1	The role of ski representative	Lead discussion on holiday experience, presentation on role and duties of ski representatives, outline activity, support	Investigate and contrast different company descriptions of role and skills of ski reps. Present findings to class	Presentations, discussion, questioning	2, 3, 4	Handouts, brochures, IT access
w/c 08 Feb **Lesson (a)** L/O 1	The role of children's representatives in summer and winter programmes	Outline activity, guide and support	Research activity contrasting roles and duties, followed by a typical day role play	Role play presentations of a typical day's activities Discussion, feedback	2, 3, 4	IT access
w/c 08 Feb **Lesson (b)** L/O 1	Responsibilities to customer, organization and suppliers	Outline tasks for Key Stage Comedy DVD, discuss, feedback	Complete DVD task sheet, prepare posters, present findings to group, take notes	Discussion and assignment outcome Presentations and feedback	2, 3, 4	Key Stage Comedy DVD and task sheet Speakers Flip chart paper Markers

Figure 2.11 Exemplar scheme of work

in Chapter 4, you can link them to the outcomes given in the specifications. Your final summative assessment may require knowledge and understanding to be built up through the course of the lessons. Therefore, you may draw on knowledge or comprehension learning objectives in earlier lessons, with analysis or evaluation being included in later lessons, all based around the same topic. Bloom's taxonomy helps to give structure and progression to lessons learning objectives.

The scheme of work will take you through to delivery of all aspects of a particular unit. However, in some circumstances you may find it possible to create an imaginative delivery of a number of units simultaneously. This is known as thematic planning.

Figure 2.12 represents a schema for a project based on the Olympics in 2012 which presents an opportunity to combine a number of units around that theme. The external boxes are units.

A topic like the Olympics lends itself to teaching travel and tourism. The central subject gives a focus for each of the unit's outcomes. It takes a great deal of planning in a meticulous manner to ensure the learning outcomes are all covered in an integrated teaching programme, but this gives real meaning to the learning situation. Taking the learning outcomes from each unit you can reassemble them in an interesting, exciting and related scheme of work. It may also offer the opportunity to team teach with colleagues.

Summary

In this chapter we have focused on the wider implications of curriculum design and the various factors that influence it. We hope that it will have given you greater insight into the ideologies that drive it and the models that derive from them and how they are mirrored in the courses and programmes that we teach. It is important to understand the difference between the product curriculum and the process curriculum because

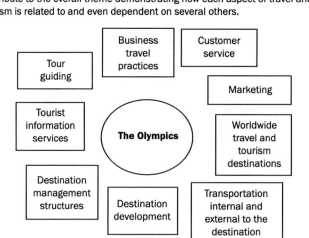

The central theme is obviously the Olympic Games 2012, but several units might contribute to the overall theme demonstrating how each aspect of travel and tourism is related to and even dependent on several others.

Figure 2.12 Designing an integrated assignment

these ideas will affect the way in which we organize the learning experiences for our students. This is the subject of the next two chapters.

If, at the end of the programme, the curriculum is to lead to more than a certificate which merely proves that certain knowledge or competence has been acquired (the product), but rather also leads to the development of the student as an independent learner with the personal skills to enter the world of employment and/or higher education (the process), then we need to plan those learning experiences very carefully and very thoroughly.

The key skills agenda which we visit in Chapter 3 addresses just these issues and seeks to seamlessly 'embed' the skills into the curriculum, which is another aspect of curriculum design that we have not really touched upon here. But the planning is only the first stage. What is most important is the face-to-face contact between teacher and learner, and this is the subject of Chapter 4, which addresses the teaching and learning experience. It is here that Stenhouse's 'reality of the curriculum' is truly experienced.

3

Embedding key skills and functional skills into the travel and tourism curriculum

In this chapter we will be looking at:

- the development of the key skills and functional skills curricula
- the main key skills and functional skills and their component parts
- barriers to learning key and functional skills
- designing learning programmes for travel and tourism that embed key and functional skills
- developing ways of supporting learners in the development of their skills
- embedding personal learning and thinking skills (PLTS) into the travel and tourism curriculum.

Introduction

Along with a concern for a perceived disaffection for schooling, as identified in the first chapter, there has been a further consistent belief that many learners have been leaving the compulsory education system ill-equipped to take a full and meaningful, independent role in society. They have been ill-equipped particularly in the skills of literacy and numeracy, but also in the more general life-skills that would make them more attractive to employers.

These concerns were reflected in the Moser Report (DfEE 1999), which 'concluded that one in five adults had literacy skills below those expected of an eleven year old' (Appleyard and Appleyard 2009: 1)

Given the implications of these alarming statistics, it is no longer acceptable for the practising teacher of travel and tourism (or teachers of any subject for that matter), to pay attention only to the content of learners' work and to ignore accuracy in use of language or of numeracy. Furthermore, in this technological age of electronic communications, it is essential that learners develop skills in information and communication technology (ICT) that enhance their ability to use such skills effectively in the wider social context beyond computer gaming and the text message.

Reflection 3.1

Figure 3.1 is an example of an assignment written by a student following a BTEC First Diploma programme in Travel and Tourism. The content seems to be acceptable, but how would you mark this in terms of the student's engagement with literacy skills? What specific problems can you identify?

While many subject teachers may lack confidence in delivering and assessing key skills or functional skills, it is now expected that they should all be able to recognize opportunities within the subject for development and assessment of these skills and, indeed, should work towards their own development in them. This is reflected in the requirements for trainee teachers on any training programme to achieve the Teachers Development Agency (TDA) standards or the minimum core in the skills. Of course, it also expected that institutions (schools, colleges and adult education centres) should provide expert advice from specialists to support subject teachers and lecturers. We shall see how this is managed when we analyse models of embedding.

So what is the proposed solution to these shortcomings? This chapter examines the background and development of the key skills and, more recently, the functional skills agenda, and will analyse the content of their curricula to enable the teacher of travel and tourism to support their learners more effectively.

Level 2 Travel and Tourism task:

Describe the appeal of different UK travel and tourism destinations for different types of visitors.

Answer:

Southend on sea appeals to a range of different customers. These have been outlined below giving reasons why Southen appeals to them:

1. Families: Southend has long been popular with familys, especially those living in nearby urban areas such as London. Southends appeal is there are good and quick tansport links to London making the journey quick and easy which is a key factor for families when making the decision of where to go on holiday or for day trips. Once families arrive in Southend there are many attractions to keep them busy from the fairground at the foot of the pier which is aimed at children to the train ride along the peer. There are many different types of arcades and the indoor entertainment centre, which once was a dance hall. There is also a Sea Life centre. All of thes attractcions are in easy walking distance of each other and offer family entrance prices. They also cater for the family in bad weather. This is appealing to family's, especially the parents as parents need to consider what there is to do for there children in bad weather, which often happens in this country!

In the summer time Southend also offers a beach area beachside cafes and gardens. These suite families and are again all in walking distance of one an other. Southend is a typical traditional British seaside resort, aimed rpimarily at the family market.

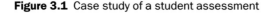

Figure 3.1 Case study of a student assessment

The background to and rise of key skills

In the 1980s programmes written by the original Business Education Council (BEC) and Technical Education Council (TEC), which later combined as the now more well-known BTEC, included an assessment of what they termed as 'common skills'. These included numeracy and literacy, and later, with the development of electronic technology, ICT.

Interestingly, BTEC policy (reflecting their learner-centred philosophy as discussed in Chapter 2) proposed that, wherever possible, these common skills should be integrated into the subject curriculum, thus ensuring that they were contextualized and made more meaningful to the learner.

This is all the more significant since BTEC pre-empted current policy which is to do precisely that – to integrate 'functional' skills wherever possible into the subject curriculum. Clearly BTEC was very conscious of the need to motivate learners by ensuring that the skills were learnt and assessed in meaningful contexts.

In the 1990s the General National Vocational Qualification was introduced. Like the BTEC programmes, this was not a qualification to actually qualify the learner to work in an industry, but was intended to be a preparation for working in specific occupations and towards eventually gaining such qualifications. Designed very much on the BTEC model, GNVQs required learners to achieve what now became known as 'key' skills, again including literacy, numeracy and ICT. They also developed a range of personal skills, which became known as the 'Wider' key skills (Working with others, Improving own learning and performance, and Problem solving), and were intended to develop skills that were seen as essential to personal, social and vocational development. The underpinning principle of the key skills agenda is that the skills should be transferable to any aspect of life and that they should be seen in the context of a coherent plan for learner development (Donovan 2005: 117).

Similar and parallel to the key skills agenda is the Adult Literacy and Numeracy (ALAN) programme which mirrors its standards and is assessed entirely by portfolio, thus ensuring that the opportunity to relate the use of the skills to real situations is possible.

Reflection 3.2

For each of the key/functional skills (Literacy/English; Numeracy/Maths; ICT) think of at least three contexts where knowledge of and competency in them is an essential asset to following a career in travel and tourism.

In fact, it is not so difficult to find such contexts in the travel and tourism industry. Communication is central to all that we do, and is essential where we are dealing with such a wide range of clients in a variety of often very challenging environments, whether advising on bookings in the agency or out in the field as a resort representative. Managing ICT is vital to our work these days from the initial bookings to designing web pages to advertise resorts and, although we may rely to an extent on electronic management of accounting, it is still essential that we can interpret the figures and make sense of them for our clients.

So it is important that we engage with the skills that are needed to run our industry and that we are familiar with them ourselves sufficiently to be able to facilitate our learners' capacity to develop them.

Following the Dearing Report (DfEE 1996), Curriculum 2000 proposed a curriculum that was intended to promote equity between the range of qualifications, whether considered academic (A levels and GCSEs) or vocational (NVQs, GNVQs, Advanced Vocational Certificate in Education [AVCE], National Diplomas) and 'key skills' at levels 1 to 4 were available to all as 'stand-alone' qualifications, incidentally, attracting UCAS points. In fact, key skills became available from Level 1 to Level 4 to learners across the education and training spectrum – including undergraduates and NVQ trainees.

Since the demise of Curriculum 2000 and the publication of the Tomlinson Report (Working Group on 14–19 Reform 2004) that proposed an integrated curriculum of diplomas (Chapters 1 and 2), the notion of 'functional skills' has been floated and, at the time of writing, they are set to replace 'key skills'.

The idea is that the essential skills should be specifically related to the learner's social and occupational environment, thus ensuring that they are seen to be relevant to their needs. Key skills were previously highly criticized for often being irrelevant and merely a repetition of GCSE Maths and English by another name. For example, what on earth would be the relevance of knowing how to calculate the volume of a cylinder to a student of travel and tourism, unless it is to check the accuracy of the contents of a soft drinks can?

So now, although the skills are assessed by a generic test, the content of the functional skills curriculum is intended to directly reflect the proposed working environment of the learner. Therefore, it should be possible to 'embed' this curriculum fully into the occupational subject curriculum. The notion of 'embedding' and the impact this has on the planning of the travel and tourism curriculum and lessons is the subject of one of the following sections.

Reflection 3.3

Consider each of the functional/key skills:

- Literacy/English
- Numeracy/Maths
- ICT

Try to think of activities taken from a travel and tourism programme on which you teach at any level, which might provide an opportunity to assess any aspect of each one.

Although it may be noticed that the 'wider' key skills appear to be missing here, the attributes that they were intended to develop are now subsumed into a programme of personal, learning and thinking skills, affectionately known as PeLTS. Again, we shall visit these later.

What are the key skills?

As we have seen, key skills are skills that are transferable from one context to another, enabling learners to develop personal effectiveness for adult and working life. As Edexcel Specifications for National Diplomas note:

> Learners need the chance to show current and future employers that they can:
>
> - communicate effectively
> - use number
> - use ICT
> - work well with others
> - manage their own development
> - solve problems.
>
> (Edexcel 2007: 305)

We shall consider these in the context of the travel and tourism industry and, of course, what this means for the development of the travel and tourism curriculum. Obviously, the skills will be developmental through each stage and we will consider each of the first three in some depth and the 'softer' skills more generally.

The following information may be found on the QCDA website (www. qcda.gov.uk accessed 8 Feb. 2010) which also gives more detail of the precise skills under each category, such as 'Interpret information: read and understand tables, charts, graphs and diagrams' (Application of number level 1).

Communication

The skills are developmental, for example, leading from simple one-to-one discussion to taking part in a group discussion, to demonstrating skill in oral communication, depending on the level (Figure 3.2, opposite). Students also have to read, comprehend and synthesize information, and write different types of documents. Communication is perhaps the easiest of the skills in which to develop opportunities for learners to demonstrate their competence. An assignment that requires the learner to read a report on a particular destination, for example, and to present a short talk on their findings would provide such opportunities for each of these aspects of communication.

Application of number

The skills in the use of number that the learner must demonstrate at the different levels (Figure 3.3) include: interpreting information from different sources, such as tables and charts; carrying out calculations to do with amounts, sizes, scales or proportion; handling statistics and using formulae; and interpreting the results of their calculations.

As we have already suggested, although it may be more difficult to find opportunities to develop the full range of skills from the travel and tourism curriculum

Level 1	Level 2	Level 3
Take part in one-to-one discussion or a group discussion	Take part in a group discussion	Take part in a group discussion
	Give a short talk	Make a formal presentation using an image or other support material
Read and obtain information	Read and summarize information	Read and synthesize information
Write two different types of documents	Write two different types of documents each one giving different information	Write two different types of documents, each one giving different information about complex subjects

Figure 3.2 Technical descriptors for key skills Communication, showing progression between levels

Level 1	Level 2	Level 3
Interpret information from two different sources	Interpret information from a suitable source	Plan an activity and get relevant information from relevant sources
Carry out and check calculations to do with amounts or sizes; scales or proportion; handling statistics	Use your information to carry out calculations to do with amounts or sizes; scales or proportion; handling statistics; using formulae	Use this information to carry out multi-stage calculations to do with amounts or sizes; scales or proportion; handling statistics; using formulae
Interpret the results of your calculations and present findings	Interpret the results of your calculations and present findings	Interpret the results of your calculations and present findings and justify your methods

Figure 3.3 Technical descriptors for key skills Application of Number showing progression between levels

such skills can be found at all levels. On the one hand, the obvious simple application would be to work out the costing of holidays or, for dealing with spacial concepts, redesigning the layout of a travel agency office. On the other hand, there are plenty of opportunities to use higher-level skills in the analysis of travel statistics.

Information and communication technology

Here the learner is required to use electronic sources to search for information for specific purposes, at higher levels using different sources and criteria. They then have to enter and develop the information before presenting it accurately and, at higher levels, combining text, images and number (Figure 3.4).

Many (though not necessarily all) young people today are familiar with modern electronic technology, although this may be largely practised in a recreational context.

Level 1	Level 2	Level 3
Find and select relevant information	Search for and select information to meet your needs.	Search for information using different sources, and multiple search criteria
Enter and develop information to suit the task	Enter and develop information to suit the task and derive new information	Enter and develop the information and derive new information
Develop the presentation so that the final output is accurate and fit for purpose	Present combined information such as text with image, text with number, image with number	Present combined information such as text with image, text with number, image with number

Figure 3.4 Technical descriptors for key skills Information and Communication Technology showing progression between levels

So the teacher's task here is to apply the standards to realistic situations that will enable their learners to develop their skills to seek out efficiently information from the vast store now available and apply them to enhance effective communication in a working environment. Again, it would not be so difficult to design opportunities for learners to demonstrate their skill in ICT through researching resort or travel information from Internet sources, for example, and then presenting their findings either in an assignment or perhaps a PowerPoint presentation.

However, it should also be remembered that, equally, many adults may be unfamiliar with, and even fearful of, technology and may need much sympathetic guidance. This we discuss later under 'Supporting learner development'.

> **Reflection 3.4**
>
> Consider the scheme of work in Figure 2.8 (Chapter 2). Using the charts in Figures 3.2, 3.3 and 3.4, try to identify activities from the travel and tourism curriculum that will help to generate evidence for any of the skills listed, or devise some of your own.

The wider key skills

Although the key skills of Communication, Numeracy and ICT are assessed by both portfolio and external test, the wider skills are assessed by portfolio alone which means that opportunities to provide evidence of their achievement can be generated during the normal course of studies. These are skills that might be described as 'process' skills since they reflect the attributes that the learner needs to develop in order to become a better learner and a more effective member of society. Managing their own development would suggest that they could learn to become more independent and take responsibility for their own learning. Solving problems is a skill that will, again, help develop autonomy, and working with others suggests that they will learn to contribute to the good of the whole and respect the contributions of others.

Reflection 3.5

With reference to the wider key skills listed in Figure 3.5 and the scheme of work in Chapter 2 (Figure 2.8), do the same exercise as in Reflection 3.4 and try to identify or create opportunities for learners to generate evidence for the wider skills.

Criterion	Working with others	Improving own learning	Problem solving
1	Understand the implications of working with others	Setting targets and devising an action plan	How to identify and solve problems
2	Identify and carry out tasks within a team	Develop strategies to improve own learning	Develop a plan to solve a problem
3	Evaluate the work of the team	Review progress and modify the action plan	Evaluate how successful the plan has been in solving the problem

Figure 3.5 Summarizing the wider skills

Adult literacy, adult numeracy and ICT skills

A number of our adult learners will possibly be working towards achievement under the Adult Literacy and Adult Numeracy programme. Launched in 2001 as part of the Government's Skills for Life Public Service agreement and in response to concern over the low levels of adult literacy and numeracy, targets were set to improve the basic skills of 2.25 million adults by 2010. The standards, set by QCDA, 'Are very closely linked to the key skills qualifications standards' and 'are technical documents intended for use by those working in education and training to form the basis of curricula, qualifications and assessment material' (QCDA 2009).

Similar to key skills, they are assessed by externally examined tests covering knowledge and understanding, but learners also have to produce a portfolio of evidence showing practical application of the skills. Some of the work carried out under your travel and tourism programmes may well form part of their portfolios of evidence, and this is something to bear in mind when planning for learning and assessment.

Reflection 3.6

As we have noted, many adults might be fearful of using ICT.

You are teaching a class of adults following an Open College Network (OCN) programme. The unit requires them to produce a poster advertising holidays for the over-50s using PowerPoint.

How might you help them to overcome this fear and develop their skills in a way that will enhance their capacity to learn?

What are functional skills?

At the time of writing, the functional skills project is still at the pilot stage of development. However, functional skills will be launched for general delivery and assessment in 2010. Although the Leitch Report (DfEE 2006) focused on addressing what was perceived as a deficit in vocational skills, undoubtedly, there was an implication that without an improvement in national standards in English, mathematics and ICT to support it, there would be little commensurate improvement overall. The challenge to 'close the skills gap' by 2020 would fail at the first hurdle, so the Government have made the development of the functional skills agenda a national priority. At the same time, this development is seen to support the Every Child Matters agenda by ensuring that all learners have the opportunity to 'gain the most out life, learning and work' (QCA 2007: 3).

> Functional skills in English, mathematics and information and communication technology (ICT) help people to gain the most out of life, learning and work.
>   The skills are learning tools that enable people:
>
> - to apply their knowledge and understanding to everyday life
> - to engage competently and confidently with others
> - to solve problems in both familiar and unfamiliar situations
> - to develop personally and professionally as positive citizens who can actively contribute to society.
>
> (QCA 2007: 3)

Functional skills, then, relate to the development of skills in English, mathematics and ICT. Note the change in descriptors from 'Communication' and 'Numeracy'. However, the rhetoric and principles remain the same as for key skills: 'The term "functional" should be considered in the broad sense of providing learners with the skills and abilities they need to take an active and responsible role in their communities, everyday life, the workplace and educational settings' (QCA 2007: 7, 19 and 27).

The specifications for each skills area are far more detailed than those for key skills and, although it is expected that functional skills should be delivered in the context of the general subject (in our case, of course, travel and tourism), they are assessed entirely by specific tests, some external and some internal.

English

'Functional English requires learners to communicate in ways that make them effective and involved citizens, to operate confidently and to convey their ideas and opinions clearly' (QCA 2007: 7).

Mathematics

'Functional Mathematics requires learners to use mathematics in ways that make them effective and involved as citizens, to operate confidently in life, and to work in a wide range of contexts' (QCA 2007: 19).

ICT

'Functional ICT requires learners to use technology in ways that make them effective and involved as citizens, to operate confidently in life, and to work in a wide range of contexts' (QCA 2007: 27).

Embedding key and functional skills into the occupational subject curriculum

The notion of embedding key skills and functional skills into the learning and teaching programme is not a new idea. Indeed, although they may not have used the current buzz word, the principle of assessing common skills through subject assignment work could be found in the BTEC Diplomas of the 1980s and 1990s and later in the GNVQs. As we have seen, key skills are now assessed not only through completion of a test but also by presentation of a portfolio in which is identified evidence of practical application of the skills. Embedding key skills means, therefore, creating or recognizing opportunities for learners to apply those skills to any other aspect of their learning programme. This might be planned by the teacher when writing the scheme of work or lesson plan, or even presented as a task for the learner to review their own work to recognize where they might identify evidence of achievement for themselves.

Essentially, then, embedding the skills is intended to create opportunities for learners to use them in realistic contexts that will make them more meaningful and thus motivate learners to develop their skills still further.

Although functional skills are examined purely through a series of tests, learning should be facilitated by embedding them in the same way into the subject programme. The tests themselves are set in realistic working environments. Figures 3.6 and 3.7, overleaf, are examples of tests related to the travel and tourism curriculum, which can be found on the Edexcel website (http://www.edexcel.com/quals/Pages/qual-home.aspx).

Supporting learner development of key and functional skills

Common problems, disabilities and learning difficulties in the key skills

As a teacher of travel and tourism, you will undoubtedly encounter a number of learners who experience difficulties with some or all of the key skills to varying degrees. As we noted in the introduction, these difficulties cannot simply be ignored in favour of the content of the subject. Indeed, they may even inhibit our learners' enjoyment and their ability to understand it. So we have a responsibility to them to be aware of any problems they may have with any of the skills and to support them in

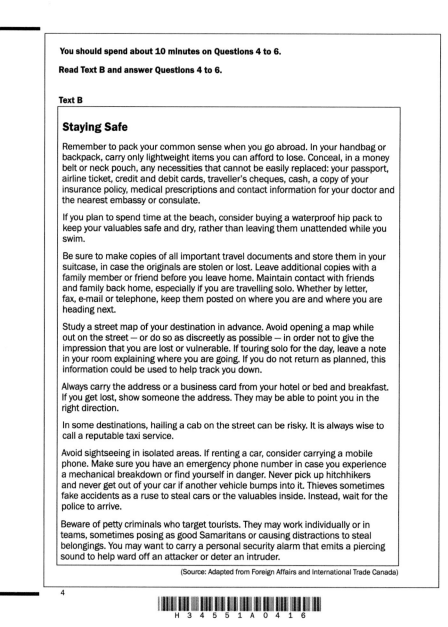

You should spend about 10 minutes on Questions 4 to 6.

Read Text B and answer Questions 4 to 6.

Text B

Staying Safe

Remember to pack your common sense when you go abroad. In your handbag or backpack, carry only lightweight items you can afford to lose. Conceal, in a money belt or neck pouch, any necessities that cannot be easily replaced: your passport, airline ticket, credit and debit cards, traveller's cheques, cash, a copy of your insurance policy, medical prescriptions and contact information for your doctor and the nearest embassy or consulate.

If you plan to spend time at the beach, consider buying a waterproof hip pack to keep your valuables safe and dry, rather than leaving them unattended while you swim.

Be sure to make copies of all important travel documents and store them in your suitcase, in case the originals are stolen or lost. Leave additional copies with a family member or friend before you leave home. Maintain contact with friends and family back home, especially if you are travelling solo. Whether by letter, fax, e-mail or telephone, keep them posted on where you are and where you are heading next.

Study a street map of your destination in advance. Avoid opening a map while out on the street — or do so as discreetly as possible — in order not to give the impression that you are lost or vulnerable. If touring solo for the day, leave a note in your room explaining where you are going. If you do not return as planned, this information could be used to help track you down.

Always carry the address or a business card from your hotel or bed and breakfast. If you get lost, show someone the address. They may be able to point you in the right direction.

In some destinations, hailing a cab on the street can be risky. It is always wise to call a reputable taxi service.

Avoid sightseeing in isolated areas. If renting a car, consider carrying a mobile phone. Make sure you have an emergency phone number in case you experience a mechanical breakdown or find yourself in danger. Never pick up hitchhikers and never get out of your car if another vehicle bumps into it. Thieves sometimes fake accidents as a ruse to steal cars or the valuables inside. Instead, wait for the police to arrive.

Beware of petty criminals who target tourists. They may work individually or in teams, sometimes posing as good Samaritans or causing distractions to steal belongings. You may want to carry a personal security alarm that emits a piercing sound to help ward off an attacker or deter an intruder.

(Source: Adapted from Foreign Affairs and International Trade Canada)

4

H 3 4 5 5 1 A 0 4 1 6

Figure 3.6 (a) and (b) Exemplar functional skills external test (pilot)

order to maximize their learning. The key skills and functional skills curricula exist as a guide to our expectations of the standards they should achieve.

It is important to acknowledge that these problems are not confined to those learners with identified disabilities and learning difficulties, but that most of our learners will need some help to improve one or two aspects of their key skills. This may be a problem with the use of the apostrophe or in giving a verbal presentation, or

	Leave blank

For Questions 1 to 3, choose an answer, A, B, C or D and put a cross in the box (☒).

Question 1

According to Text A, your insurance policy might not cover you if:

A   you are injured after drinking alcohol   ☐

B   you do not have a European Health Insurance Certificate   ☐

C   you bought your insurance by credit card   ☐

D   you are in a remote location   ☐   Q1

(Total 1 mark)

Question 2

According to Text A, which of these statements is correct?

A   Many people don't take out travel insurance because it is too expensive.   ☐

B   Travel insurance is unnecessary if you have private health cover.   ☐

C   Insurers will not insure you if you have previously been ill.   ☐

D   It is better for frequent travellers to insure themselves for a year.   ☐   Q2

(Total 1 mark)

Question 3

The main purpose of Text A is to:

A   warn readers about the dangers of going on holiday   ☐

B   explain to readers where to buy travel insurance   ☐

C   persuade readers to buy travel insurance   ☐

D   advise readers how to avoid injuries on holiday   ☐   Q3

(Total 1 mark)

with converting currencies, or with saving and editing documents. A good starting point would be diagnostic assessments that identify individual strengths and areas for further development so that we can plan sessions that present opportunities to develop learners' skills or modify our own teaching to make it more accessible for them.

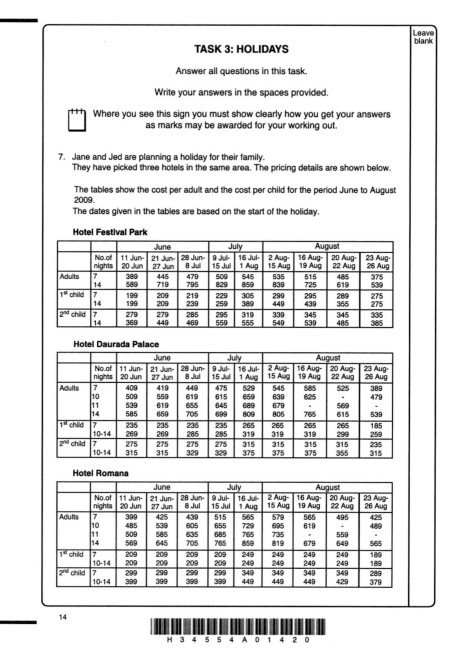

TASK 3: HOLIDAYS

Answer all questions in this task.

Write your answers in the spaces provided.

Where you see this sign you must show clearly how you get your answers as marks may be awarded for your working out.

7. Jane and Jed are planning a holiday for their family.
    They have picked three hotels in the same area. The pricing details are shown below.

    The tables show the cost per adult and the cost per child for the period June to August 2009.
    The dates given in the tables are based on the start of the holiday.

Hotel Festival Park

	No.of nights	June 11 Jun-20 Jun	21 Jun-27 Jun	28 Jun-8 Jul	July 9 Jul-15 Jul	16 Jul-1 Aug	August 2 Aug-15 Aug	16 Aug-19 Aug	20 Aug-22 Aug	23 Aug-26 Aug
Adults	7	389	445	479	509	545	535	515	485	375
	14	589	719	795	829	859	839	725	619	539
1st child	7	199	209	219	229	305	299	295	289	275
	14	199	209	239	259	389	449	439	355	275
2nd child	7	279	279	285	295	319	339	345	345	335
	14	369	449	469	559	555	549	539	485	385

Hotel Daurada Palace

	No.of nights	June 11 Jun-20 Jun	21 Jun-27 Jun	28 Jun-8 Jul	July 9 Jul-15 Jul	16 Jul-1 Aug	August 2 Aug-15 Aug	16 Aug-19 Aug	20 Aug-22 Aug	23 Aug-26 Aug
Adults	7	409	419	449	475	529	545	585	525	389
	10	509	559	619	615	659	639	625	-	479
	11	539	619	655	645	689	679	-	569	-
	14	585	659	705	699	809	805	765	615	539
1st child	7	235	235	235	235	265	265	265	265	185
	10-14	269	269	285	285	319	319	319	299	259
2nd child	7	275	275	275	275	315	315	315	315	235
	10-14	315	315	329	329	375	375	375	355	315

Hotel Romana

	No.of nights	June 11 Jun-20 Jun	21 Jun-27 Jun	28 Jun-8 Jul	July 9 Jul-15 Jul	16 Jul-1 Aug	August 2 Aug-15 Aug	16 Aug-19 Aug	20 Aug-22 Aug	23 Aug-26 Aug
Adults	7	399	425	439	515	565	579	565	495	425
	10	485	539	605	655	729	695	619	-	489
	11	509	585	635	685	765	735	-	559	-
	14	569	645	705	765	859	819	679	649	565
1st child	7	209	209	209	209	249	249	249	249	189
	10-14	209	209	209	209	249	249	249	249	189
2nd child	7	299	299	299	299	349	349	349	349	289
	10-14	399	399	399	399	449	449	449	429	379

14

Figure 3.7 (a) and (b) Exemplar functional skills external test (pilot)

As teachers we need to ensure that our own skills and our understanding of language, number and ICT are sufficiently honed to be able to identify where there are problems and to be able to deal with them (Appleyard and Appleyard 2009: 7). Perhaps the first activity should be to try out a diagnostic assessment task for ourselves!

Leave blank

Jane and Jed have two children.
They want to book a 14 night holiday starting on 10th August.

They also need to arrange holiday insurance and a taxi to and from Manchester Airport.

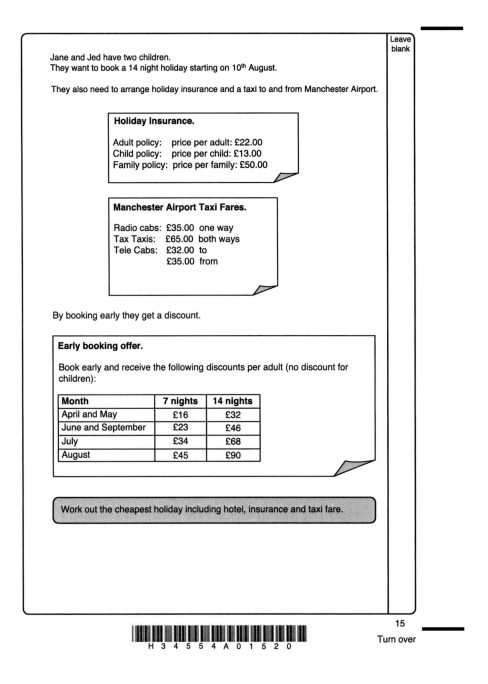

Holiday Insurance.

Adult policy: price per adult: £22.00
Child policy: price per child: £13.00
Family policy: price per family: £50.00

Manchester Airport Taxi Fares.

Radio cabs: £35.00 one way
Tax Taxis: £65.00 both ways
Tele Cabs: £32.00 to
            £35.00 from

By booking early they get a discount.

Early booking offer.

Book early and receive the following discounts per adult (no discount for children):

Month	7 nights	14 nights
April and May	£16	£32
June and September	£23	£46
July	£34	£68
August	£45	£90

Work out the cheapest holiday including hotel, insurance and taxi fare.

H 3 4 5 5 4 A 0 1 5 2 0

You might wish to revisit Reflection 3.1, completed earlier in the chapter, as a check on your own familiarity with the key skills.

Reflection 3.7

Can you identify any specific problems for the learner in Figure 3.1?

How could you help them to address their problems?

Who might you consult if you felt that this was beyond your own expertise?

Of course, each of the key skills subjects brings its own specific problems, but there are also some that are generic that may be generated by common 'barriers to learning'.

Generic barriers to learning key skills

Armitage et al. (2007) identify three main categories of barriers to learning: we would do well to briefly examine these in relation to the problems that learners may have with key skills. They may be categorized as educational, which implies that the learner has either specific difficulties or low motivation to learn; institutional, where the school or college may have not given sufficient support to the learner; and societal, which places the problems in the context of the learner's role in, and relationship with, society as a whole.

Reflection 3.8

What do you think are the barriers that the learners in Figure 3.8 might face? How might their teachers help them to overcome the barriers?

Consider the following case studies: what 'barriers' to effective learning might they encounter?

Jane is a 17-year-old who left school a year ago with three very low-grade GCSEs. Although she was disruptive at school, she has been talking to some friends who have just completed a First Diploma in Travel and Tourism at the local college. Realizing that she will need to get qualifications for work, she has reluctantly been persuaded also to enrol on the BTEC First Diploma programme for the next year.

Kathy is a 30-year-old mother of two who left school at 16. Although she worked for a few years as a shop assistant, she has spent most of her married life looking after the family. In her mid-twenties she developed an interest in travel and tourism and now has enrolled on an access programme intending to make a new career. Her husband has just been made redundant and is looking for a new career too.

James is 19 and left the local FE college with a BTEC National in Travel and Tourism. He has worked in a pub at weekends and in the holidays and, although he's not sure exactly what kind of career he wants to follow, he is about to start a Foundation Degree in Hospitality and Institutional Management at university. His parents are unable to give him much financial support.

Figure 3.8 Case studies of barriers to learning

The point that Armitage et al. make here is that, although these barriers might well be considered as separate causes of a learner's barriers to their competence in the key skills, they are most probably interlinked. Problems with sentence structure, for example, might have arisen from a lack of opportunities to read quality literature at home or from a poor relationship with a teacher at school, or both. The former could be considered societal while the latter could be educational and/or institutional. But it is helpful to consider these categories when we try to understand the issues facing particular learners if we are to be able to help them. Indeed, in the context of the Every Child (Learner) Matters policy, it is essential.

Some specific disabilities and learning difficulties

There is insufficient space in this publication to consider these in depth, and in any case that is really the task of more specialist books such as the Minimum Core series published by Learning Matters (in 2009). Clearly, if teachers do encounter identified, or even suspected, problems as severe as this, they should seek the advice of specialist support teachers. Nevertheless, as we have previously noted, learners with such problems will be members of our classes and we should be prepared to adapt our teaching accordingly.

The list of specific difficulties includes:

- deaf or partially hearing learners
- blind or partially sighted learners
- learners with mental health problems
- learners with dyslexia
- learners with physical disabilities
- learners with learning difficulties
- learners with autistic spectrum disorder.

The ability of learners in each category to engage with the key and functional skills may be challenged to varying degrees of severity and, of course, since we are concerned with the whole of the lifelong learning sector, we should perhaps also bear in mind that ageing may exacerbate some of those problems, relating for example to hearing and sight. However, there are strategies that can be adopted to alleviate the problems that these learners encounter, or at least to try to ensure that they do not find the learning challenging purely because of their disability. To this extent, and in the spirit of Every Child (Learner) Matters, we should ensure that the learning is personalized for them, in particular.

Clearly, first, we might hope that there would be a learning assistant available and you should discuss your lesson and the possible strategies that would be most appropriate with them well before the lesson. But you, too, can plan to accommodate such learners:

- Make sure that you speak clearly and, if necessary, be aware that some may need to lip-read.

- Give clear information and instructions.
- Repeat yourself and provide visual stimuli (handouts or PowerPoint).
- Break down tasks into manageable components.
- Use coloured paper for handouts, particularly an issue for dyslexia sufferers.
- Customize ICT systems using the Accessibility options.
- Adapt keyboards.
- Use voice input software.
- Ensure that the learners have a safe environment in which to work. This is particularly important for those with autistic spectrum disorders (ASD).
       (Appleyard and Appleyard 2009; Clarke 2006; Delaney 2009; Peart 2009)

Reflection 3.9

Consider the scheme of work in Chapter 2 (Figure 2.8).

What adaptations might you need to make for learners with dyscalculia, dyslexia or ASD in your travel and tourism lessons?

Personal learning and thinking skills

Earlier in this chapter we mentioned 'wider key skills', which became a part of the GNVQ and National Diploma curriculum. Interestingly, these seem to have been revived under the title of 'Personal learning and thinking skills' associated with the new 14–19 Diplomas discussed in Chapter 2. It is worth noting that employers, represented by sector skills councils, played a major role in developing the diplomas and specifically in identifying those skills that they felt were most useful in the workplace. There is a fairly common belief among teachers and trainers who have been delivering vocational programmes that employers often have been more interested in the general abilities of prospective employees, such as the ability to work with others, to show initiative and to learn new skills, than the actual qualification with which they leave full-time education. In the spirit of the Leitch Report that recommended greater levels of engagement of employers in the development of learning programmes, they were invited to help to develop a curriculum that reflected their concerns and which would enable learners to develop and demonstrate these skills.

So what are these PLTS? Figure 3.9 presents a summary of the main themes and what particular skills are associated with each one and, from this, it may be clearly seen that they are intended to indentify aspects of personal development that will enable the learner to become a more rounded and independent individual. As already noted, these have been developed as an important aspect of the 14–19 Diplomas, but there are components of this qualification that might be studied independently of the main programme, as 'stand-alone' qualifications, notably the individual project which carries the value of half an A level, that is five credits at level 3 (see Chapter 2

Creative thinkers
a) Generate ideas and explore possibilities
b) Ask questions to extend thinking
c) Connect their own and others' ideas and experiences in inventive ways
d) Question their own and others' assumptions
e) Try out alternative or new solutions and follow ideas through
f) Adapt ideas as circumstances change

Independent enquirers
a) Identify questions to answer and problems to resolve
b) Plan and carry out research, appreciating the consequences of decisions
c) Explore issues, events or problems from different perspectives
d) Analyse and evaluate information, judging its relevance and value
e) Consider the influence of circumstances, beliefs and feelings on decisions and events
f) Support conclusions, using reasoned arguments and evidence

Reflective learners
a) Assess themselves and others, identifying opportunities and achievements
b) Set goals with success criteria for development and work
c) Review progress, acting on outcomes
d) Invite feedback and deal positively with praise, setbacks and criticism
e) Evaluate experiences and learning to inform future progress
f) Communicate their learning in relevant ways for different audiences

Team workers
a) Collaborate with others to work towards common goals
b) Reach agreements, managing discussions to achieve results
c) Adapt behaviour to suit different roles and situations, including leadership roles
d) Show fairness and consideration to others
e) Take responsibility, showing confidence in themselves and their contribution
f) Provide constructive support and feedback to others

Self managers
a) Seek out challenges or new responsibilities and show flexibility when priorities change
b) Work towards goals, showing initiative, commitment and perseverance
c) Organize time and resources, prioritizing actions
d) Anticipate, take and manage risk
e) Deal with competing pressures, including personal and work-related demands
f) Respond positively to change, seeking advice and support when needed
g) Manage their emotions, and build and maintain relationships

Effective participators
a) Discuss issues of concern, seeking resolution where needed
b) Present a persuasive case for action
c) Propose practical ways forward, breaking these down into manageable steps
d) Identify improvements that would benefit others as well as themselves
e) Try to influence others, negotiating and balancing diverse views to reach workable solutions
f) Act as an advocate for views and beliefs that may differ from your own

Figure 3.9 Summary of the personal, learning and thinking skills (PLTS)

for an explanation of the credit framework). Indeed, at least one university preparing postgraduate trainees for teaching has focused on developing PLTS as a component of the general curriculum. So we can, perhaps, expect to see further developments in this area.

Reflection 3.10

Figure 3.10 is a case study of a learner researching for her extended project as a part of her Diploma in Travel and Tourism.

Can you identify which aspects of personal learning and thinking skills she can provide evidence for in this activity?

Anna is taking the Advanced Diploma in Travel and Tourism and, with her fellow students, is faced with the challenge of researching the potential for tourism development in her local town. Anna persuades her 'team' that they will need to engage in a market research programme to find out (a) views on existing facilities from visitors to the town and (b) the views of local residents on increased tourism activity. She researches the local town council offices and groups meeting in the local community to find out whom they might approach.

Anna is being instrumental in making her suggestion – she is keen to investigate as preparation for her extended project, which is about the diversity of visitors to the town. She therefore has an interest in identifying the most appropriate sources for her own purposes down the line. As a final outcome of her project, she is planning to give a presentation with her recommendations to the local tourism department.

Figure 3.10 Identifying PLTS in a diploma extended project

Embedding PLTS in the travel and tourism curriculum

As with functional skills, it is intended that PLTS should be fully embedded into the wider curriculum. Indeed, aspects of the 14–19 Diploma curriculum have been specifically developed with this in mind, as we can see from Reflection 3.10. But, as has already been discussed in Chapter 2, a main principle of diploma delivery is learning through applied learning strategies, such as practical, occupationally relevant activities, and through an assessed work placement. So when planning a curriculum through a scheme of work and lesson plans, it is important to identify opportunities to develop and assess the achievement of PLTS.

Reflection 3.11

The exemplar lesson plan in Figure 3.11 identifies opportunities to develop PLTS in the preamble, notably 'Improving one's learning,' and 'Problem solving'.

Can you identify the points in the lesson where this might be possible?

Using the information in Figure 3.9, what other personal learning and thinking skills might be developed through this lesson plan?

Achievement might then be recorded, perhaps using one of the useful charts published by the various examination boards.

THE BLACKPOOL
Sixth Form College

Tutor: Z Slater	Subject & Level: BTEC First Travel and Tourism	Group: First Diploma
Date: 14/05/09	Session: 5	Room: W116

On Register: Male: 1   Female: 2

Main Aims of the Lesson: This lesson is a continuation of the previous session based on the P4 criteria of unit 8. The learners are in the process of putting together their own itinerary for a trip to Alton Towers as evidence for this unit.

Learning Outcomes: *What should students be able to do?*
1) **Determine** the main topics that need considering when planning an itinerary
2) **Explain** why each of these factors needs considering
3) **Research** into the appropriate information needed to complete our itineraries.
4) **Examine** if the itinerary planned meets the aims of the trips
5) **Complete** the itinerary

Directed Study Tasks (Homework) Set: *Tasks set for completion outside of lesson time.*
Previous Directed Study: Learners previous lesson was session 2 today and therefore no directed study was set yet: it will be set in this session.

Directed Study from this lesson: To produce a paragraph (approx 10 sentences) on why you ALL needed to work effectively to organise the trip. **Stretch** to give examples when and how you all did, as well as the effects of not working effectively can have?

Homework: To finish typing up the content of the lesson for submission on 18th May as well as add to their diaries regarding the planning for this trip.

E-Learning / ILT:
Students are to use the Internet for research into the information that goes into their itinerary i.e suitable transport/costs. They will further use laptops to type up their assessment work (also used in their homework) with the promotion of e-learning using Google docs. The promethean board will be used to create checklist and to display answers to the starter activity. If need be students can email organisations to find costs and will do so in a professional manner so building up on their literacy skills also.

Differentiation and Stretch: *Include reference to the organisation of any group work*
Differentiation will occur from the directed study task where students will be given a certain number of points that they need to have thought of which will be based on their progress grade and also on which topics to cover in the directed study task – although all are encouraged to achieve the higher grades. **Stretch** will also be used when asking learners to explain their answers and reasoning therefore, **differentiation via questioning** will occur, with more able students being asked to contribute answers to more complex questions. **Differentiation** from resources will be used as students can use a range of guide-books, text books, websites, brochures to find out the needed information. Learners will further be stretched and supported in the individual time when students are completing the task and teacher is to check learning.

Resources used:
Laptops for write up of task.
Internet for research
Promethean Board
Guide books/brochures (if learners chosen brochure is found in them)
Post its

Copyright: The Blackpool Sixth Form College

Every Child Matters	Key Skills / LLN
~**Enjoy & Achieve** Students will work both independently & in small groups **(enjoy)** to complete tasks set, resulting in knowledge gained **(achieve)** **Enjoyment** can be classed as students have taken responsibility and chosen an attraction that they would like to go to themselves. ~**Stay Safe:** Discussion allows scope to consider the safety of the attractions visited and the transport used. ~**Positive Contribution** group tasks in contributing to the spider diagram & feedback allow each student to contribute to class learning –**Eating Healthy** will be promoted to learners through their choice of food establishments to be visited during their itinerary.	– Group work helps develop learners' ability to **work with others** – Pair and group work and feeding back to the rest of the group contributes to developing **communication** skills. – Research into finding costs, opening times to support their assessment work help develop **ILT** skills along with typing up their assignment work. – **Literacy/Language** is developed from learners' reading different sources of text to extract the information they need. – **Numeracy** skills will be encouraged through timed activities as well as students having to work out timings and also staying within a reasonable budget so all can attend. – **Improving ones learning** – students read own work and evaluate to give self a target to improve on. – **Problem solving** – Students will have to solve problems including going over budget, no availability, timing issues etc

Time	Tutor Input	Student Activities: *What students are doing, how they are being organised*	Assessment of learning during the lesson
2 mins	**Introduction to the topic –** Tutor will display and discuss the topic objectives	**WHAT – WE are here to** – Students will take down key details of the session, to include objectives and proposed outcomes	
5 mins	**Students** to fill in alphabet box regarding what needs considering for the itinerary.	Each student to complete the alphabet box on what needs considering for the itinerary (remind them of P3) and then to collate on the board. **Stretch** to explain why it needs considering.	**Answers given in the grid and explanation stated.** (objective 1,2)
5 mins		Students to reduce the list to the key points that need putting in their itinerary.	**Reduced list generated** (objective 1,2)
5 mins		Students then to consider 'how are they considering their aims?' and 'why they have considered their aims' – aims may need displaying on the board.	**Answers given in discussion and outcome of assessment work** (objective 2,3,4)
10 mins		Students to each be designated an aim and on post-it to state how their itinerary so far meets this aim.	
25 mins	**Preparing for assessment –** Tutor to individually circulate and check learning and providing questions to support and stretch learners (EAL to have further support with English skills)	Students to continue working on their itinerary individually. Tutor to provide individual support. Students to check on work against the checklist to check all has been included and give mark out of 5 for their assignment work – how could they improve? Is it suitable?	**Content of assessment paragraph** (objective 1,2,3,4,5)
10 mins	Peer marking	If time to peer assess (which will help with EAL learner)	**Self marking scores and peer marking and lists added on to work for learner to add to in own time.** (objective, 1,2,3,4,5)

5 mins	Is this a good or bad itinerary? Why? Does it meet their aims?	To use the itinerary projected on the board to discuss whether it is a good itinerary or not? Why? And how it can be improved – can circle aspects on the board. **Stretch:** does it meet their aims	**Ideas given, answers given and markings on the board.** (objective 1,4,5)
3 mins	**Directed Study** – working effectively in preparation for M2	**Directed Study from this lesson**: To produce a paragraph (approx 10 sentences) on why you ALL needed to work effectively to organise the trip. **Stretch** to give examples when and how you all did, as well as the effects of not working effectively can have?	**Content of final assessment work.** (objective 1,2,3,4,5)
	Homework: Continue with write up.	**Homework**: To finish typing up the content of the lesson for submission on 18th May as well as add to their diaries regarding the planning for this trip.	**Content of final assessment work.** (objective 1,2,3,4,5)
Evaluation:			

Figure 3.11 Embedding PLTS into the travel and tourism lesson plan

As an exercise you might like to try to review the exemplar lesson plan in Chapter 4, Figure 4.8, and try to identify the opportunities for developing and assessing PLTS.

Summary

The key skills agenda has its origins in the New Vocationalism movement of the 1980s which sought to promote higher levels of literacy, numeracy and ICT skills in order to develop the economic progress of the UK. We have seen how this has underpinned many programmes of learning since that time and how key skills are about re-emerge as functional skills.

In this concern for the economic well-being of the nation, we must not underestimate the value to the individual of developing the skills. Not only may this make them more employable, but perhaps it will help them to be more confident in this age where it can be hard to keep up with the rapid growth of technology.

We have identified how many people have set up barriers to developing their skills: barriers which may have been formed at school or college, or perhaps in their social lives. Some may have special inherent difficulties with learning the skills, and we must be able to identify these and seek out specialist help where necessary. But we must also be aware of our own barriers to the skills and seek to improve our knowledge and understanding of them.

Here we have tried to show how we can make the development of the skills more meaningful by contextualizing them, embedding them into our travel and tourism curriculum, so that the learners are not just going over the same old maths and English that they did at school, but really see that the skills can have a purpose in their everyday working lives. This is the why we now talk about 'functional skills': they are skills that we can really use and actually need in order to develop in our chosen occupation.

Our next chapter is concerned with developing strategies for effective learning. Arguably, effective learning is underpinned by a certain level of proficiency in the key and functional skills and, as teachers, we need to be able to recognize where our learners may be struggling with these skills and support them so that they can gain higher levels of satisfaction from the learning experience.

4

Learning and teaching in the travel and tourism curriculum

At the end of this chapter the reader should be able to:

- identify the diversity of learners to be found in the life-long learning sector who might wish to study travel and tourism as a vocational subject
- identify the needs and aspirations of these different groups of learners
- define the characteristics of effective learning in the context of the travel and tourism curriculum
- develop strategies that will promote effective learning in this context
- design and plan lessons in travel and tourism studies that will promote effective learning.

Introduction

We have seen in Chapter 2 how the objectives and design of the many varied programmes on offer to the would-be student of travel and tourism reflect some very specific philosophies or ideologies of education. We also saw how these, in turn, can influence the way in which the subject might be studied or taught. If we wish to train someone to operate a ticketing system efficiently, then we need to design a programme that will enable them to develop the necessary techniques on which the system is based. But is there more to it than this? Does the operator need to understand and respond to the customer's needs, for example? On the other hand, would the kind of programme designed for the aspiring travel consultant need to be more sophisticated? They would, perhaps, need to make intuitive judgements about their client's needs and limitations in order to assess the suitability of available destinations.

How can we effectively help learners to develop such techniques, knowledge and understanding? To what extent do we need to consider the different life experiences, ages and aspirations of the learners themselves when designing our learning programmes?

This is the very essence of this chapter which first reviews the nature of the wide variety of learners to be found in the lifelong learning sector as discussed in Chapter 1; then, considering the objectives of the different learning programmes in travel and tourism, we suggest appropriate strategies and methods to promote effective learning; this leads us to develop lesson plans that will enable us to create meaningful learning experiences.

Learners in the lifelong learning (14+) sector: who are our learners?

In Chapter 1, we considered the nature and expectations of the younger adult compared with the mature adult. Bearing in mind the 'cautionary note' about generalizations, we can briefly summarize these characteristics. Many of our young adults may come to us with at least some knowledge and understanding relevant to travel and tourism either through aspects of the National Curriculum, or through having taken a GCSE in Leisure and Tourism or at least through family holidays.

Possibly their experiences will have painted a very attractive picture of the industry and they may have unrealistic expectations of what it actually means to work in travel and tourism. Coupled with a background of adolescent behavioural development, this can present very definite challenges to the teacher. On the other hand, it is normally expected that the more mature learner will have determined the career path that they wish to follow, will have carefully chosen their programme of study and will have rather more realistic expectations.

Malcolm Knowles, in his work on the adult learner (1984), identified their characteristics and Figure 4.1 provides a useful comparison with younger learners. He went on to suggest that such differences require different approaches to learning and teaching, and described the approach to be taken with adults as andragogical, as opposed to how we might plan to teach younger learners who are either still a part of the compulsory education phase, or within two or three years of this, which he described as pedagogical.

	Pedagogical	**Andragogical**
Concept of the learner	Dependent personality	Increasingly self-directed
Role of the learner's experience	To be built on, more than used a resource	A rich resource for learning by self and other
Reading to learn	Uniform by age, level and curriculum	Develops from life tasks and problems
Orientation to learning	Subject centred	Task or problem centred
Motivation	By external rewards and punishments	By internal incentives and curiosity

Figure 4.1 The assumptions of andragogy (Armitage et al. 2007: 79)

Reflection 4.1

Using the chart in Figure 4.1, with reference to Knowles's ideas, how might you intro-duce a travel geography lesson to a class of 16-year-olds?

How might your approach differ for a class of more mature adults of mixed experi-ence?

Knowles's work has been much criticized, and he himself eventually acknow-ledged that his andragogical approach might be appropriate, not just for adults, but for all learners: it will become clear from our preferred approaches to teaching and learning that we would concur with this latter view.

Identifying learner needs: learning styles and personalized learning

Every Child (Learner) Matters

The Every Child Matters agenda was briefly mentioned in Chapter 1, but it is an agenda that has had a huge impact on the school environment and, therefore, is one that we must consider at least for our age 14–16 learners. Indeed, it has found credibility in many institutes of post-compulsory education as 'Every Learner Matters'.

Formulated as a Green Paper in 2003, Every Learner Matters proposed five main objectives for every child: being healthy, staying safe, enjoying and achieving, making a positive contribution and economic well-being. However, it is the focus on achievement by the individual that has had considerable impact on the curriculum, particularly on the development of the notion of personalized learning.

You can find out more about Every Child Matters on the DCFS website (www.dcsf.gov.uk/everychildmatters), but what, then, does it mean to 'personalize learning'? One thing it does not mean is that the teacher needs to plan a separate lesson for each learner in her class! That would surely lead to the road to disillusion-ment for the teacher.

> while meeting everyone's needs sounds compassionate and learner-centred it is pedagogically unsound and psychologically demoralizing. (The teacher knows that clinging to this assumption will only cause her to carry around a permanent burden of guilt at her inability to live up to this impossible task).
>
> (Brookfield 1998: 133)

What we do mean by personalized learning is that we first acknowledge that each of our learners has had different life experiences and may learn in ways that are different from others. As effective teachers of travel and tourism we try to remain aware of this and respond to individual learners appropriately. So what are these differences that our learners may bring to the classroom?

We have already considered some of these in Chapter 1 and in the discussion above, where we noted the differences between young and mature learners. Chapter 3, focused on levels of ability in the key and functional skills and on barriers to learning. So, to plan effective learning activities, we need to make judgements about their needs. Clearly, in the first instance we might generalize their expectations from the type of programme on which they have enrolled. As already discussed, this would range from level 1 introductory programmes, to highly technical, advanced professional qualifications. In turn, the approach that we would take would be very different for each group of learners. We would also take into account their different ages and experiences. As we have seen above, someone who has been a regular traveller for a number of years and has planned their own holiday packages, would probably have very clear ideas on how to run a booking system and what kind of advice to give a client, compared with a young aspiring learner who may have limited experience of travel.

Learning styles

However, there is more to personalizing learning than referring to these very simplistic categories. Many theorists and researchers have suggested that people prefer to learn in different ways: that they have preferred 'learning styles'. In all, Coffield et al. (2004) have identified 71 different 'learning styles inventories' which are supposed to categorize learners according to their preferred ways of learning. In their highly critical work they claim that, out of all these inventories, just 13 may be classified as 'major models'. The two that appear to be most frequently referred to in initial teacher training are Honey and Mumford's (1992), which has a strong affinity to Kolb's (1984) experiential learning model, and the VARK inventory which identifies preferences for visual, auditory, read-write or kinaesthetic learning.

Harkin et al. (2001: 43) show the Honey and Mumford–Kolb relationship very clearly and we shall revisit the experiential learning model later (Figure 4.2), but the well known inventory identifies learners as 'activists', 'reflectors', 'theorists' or 'pragmatists'. For a full commentary on these styles there is ample literature, from the original Honey and Mumford *Manual of Learning Styles* (1992) to Harkin et al. referred to above, but in general the terms are self explanatory. Some people prefer an active learning style, others are, perhaps, more reflective or prefer to theorize, while still others might take a more practical outlook to their learning.

The VARK model, developed by Flemming (2001), suggests that preferences are related to sensory factors and this simple model is probably the one that is most commonly found in schools and colleges. The initial assessment is simple to administer, and it is relatively easy to embed learning activities to cater for these different preferences into a lesson plan. It is, therefore, a very convenient model to adopt.

However, Coffield et al. are highly critical of the inventories that are designed to categorize learners, in the first place, on the grounds that the tests seem to be highly subjective and often lacking in reliability and validity, and, second, that they tend to stereotype learners, leading to the ever-present danger of our old enemy, the 'self-fulfilling prophecy'.

Whether we can claim that any one student learns better in one way or another or not, it would seem that what we can learn from this is that there are different ways of learning and that by incorporating them all into our lessons, we can ensure

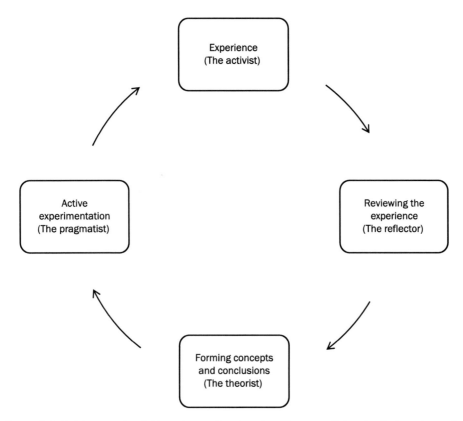

Figure 4.2 Kolb's experiential learning cycle related to Honey and Mumford's learning styles (after Harkin et al. 2001: 43)

that each learner will find a way to engage in the lesson and that, by doing so, we are reinforcing learning in different way to the benefit of all our learners. This is an important principle that we shall review when it comes to lesson planning later in the chapter.

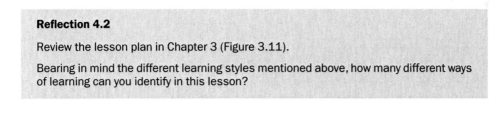

Reflection 4.2

Review the lesson plan in Chapter 3 (Figure 3.11).

Bearing in mind the different learning styles mentioned above, how many different ways of learning can you identify in this lesson?

Developing effective learning in the travel and tourism curriculum

Chapter 2 examined the various curricula available to our learners so you should be familiar with the subject matter with which they will be required to engage. This could range from simply identifying the tourist attractions in a locality to analysing the World Tourism Organization's policy documents, or from simple customer service practice to reviewing the demographic of attendees at an event. Clearly the approach one would take for different topics would vary accordingly.

The types of knowledge and skills required for these different topics have been analysed by philosophers and educationists for centuries, but one succinct 'taxonomy' that has proved to be popular and with which you may already be familiar, is that proposed by Benjamin Bloom (1964). Knowledge was identified under three basic 'domains of learning': cognitive, affective and psychomotor. Figure 4.3 shows the characteristics of each domain: the importance for our planning is that it raises our awareness and helps us to plan ways of developing learning in each domain.

Cognitive domain	Affective domain	Psychomotor domain
Evaluation	Characterizing	Naturalization
Synthesis	Organizing	Articulation
Analysis	Valuing	Precision
Application	Responding	Manipulation
Comprehension	Receiving	Imitation
Knowledge		

Figure 4.3 Major categories in each of Bloom's domains of learning (after Reece and Walker 2007: 54–6)

However, the one thing that most topics in the travel and tourism curriculum have in common is that they are grounded in practical experience, and that provides us with unique opportunities to develop a meaningful learning environment.

Ways of learning: what makes learning effective?

'Making teaching work is all about making learning happen' say Phil Race and Ruth Pickford (2007: 9) and the gist of what follows suggests ways in which we, as teachers of travel and tourism, can enable that. If we want our learners, whoever they are, to be actively engaged in an effective learning process, we do need to examine the principles that underpin that process so that we ensure that our planning takes those principles into account.

The first and most obvious question to ask appears to be 'What does it mean to learn something?' This is not necessarily a simple question to answer. Do we mean that the learner merely has to memorize facts and regurgitate them at some future date when questioned, say in an examination? Or does it mean that they should be able to make sense of the information so that they can discuss and make use of it in an appropriate situation? These are the kinds of questions that educationalists have wrestled with for centuries and which have led to the rise of many theories of learning. Here we will visit them briefly in an attempt to show how they might each influence the way we teach and plan for teaching.

The behaviourist school of learning

Returning to our first simple example above, we might recognize this as having elements of a fairly traditional approach to learning and teaching where the teacher is the fount of all knowledge who will pass this on to the learner who, having no knowledge of the subject (the Tabula Rasa), will be filled with what the teacher has selected as 'useful knowledge'. Paulo Freire (1970), the revolutionary Brazilian educator, described this as 'banking education': the teacher being the 'bank of knowledge' topping up the learner's knowledge account. The advantage of this way of teaching is that it can easily be tested. Thus, learning 'behaviour', such as memorizing facts, can be measured in a way that will satisfy the 'behaviourist' school of learning theorists. This may well have its uses when learning important data, but has serious limitations: it might help us to remember the countries of Europe, but tells us little about the theories of destination development.

The cognitivist school of learning

The cognitivist school of learning theory, on the other hand, believes that learning is a developmental process of the intellect and that, therefore, learning should be structured to lead the learner from existing knowledge to new knowledge. Clearly this too has implications for how we plan our lessons: a lesson on customer service delivery, for example, might well begin with asking learners to recall how they might have been served in various situations and to share this with the rest of the group, comparing their experiences, leading on to analysing these experiences for common factors and synthesizing a code of good practice.

The humanist school of learning

Both of the above theories assume that the teacher makes all the decisions and is central to the learning process. But yet another movement developed during the twentieth century and became a major contributor to the field of education. This was the humanist approach which values what learners bring to the learning environment and places them firmly at the centre of the process. The interaction between the teacher and the learner is essential, and this approach has generated a number of methods and strategies to foster or 'facilitate' learning. John Dewey (1963, 1974, in Harkin et al. 2001: 37–8) was a pioneer of these approaches which led initially to the development of 'project methods' that have influenced the primary school curriculum for decades, but which have also underpinned the coursework-based approach designed to encourage learner-centred research as favoured by BTEC and the National Diploma programmes. We will examine more of these as particularly appropriate ways for learning in travel and tourism.

Reflection 4.3

Figure 2.8 in Chapter 2 gives the learning outcomes in a module on marketing travel and tourism products and services.

Look up the unit content for this outcome and decide how you might teach this according to each of the learning theories: behaviourist, cognitivist and humanist.

What would be the most effective way?

For the behaviourist style you might have decided present a list of the factors to your class and ask them to learn them in preparation for a test, while the cognitive approach would see you analysing each factor and structuring the learning around question and answer strategies. The humanist, however, would certainly engage the class in question and answer perhaps to introduce the topic and to stimulate responses from the learners but they would then be set tasks to identify and research the factors in some depth and to come up with recommendations for destination development. Which do you think would have the greatest impact on the learners?

Deep and surface learning

Ways of learning that stimulate learners to learn independently of the teacher, to research information, to analyse and solve complex problems lead to 'deep learning' that is more meaningful and long-lasting. Conversely, those which demand that they merely learn facts in order to pass a test or examination, facts which might just as easily be forgotten, are thought to encourage only 'surface learning' (Gibbs 1992). Figure 4.4 illustrates the comparative characteristics of deep and surface learning.

If we are to achieve deep learning with our learners, which does seem to be the preferable option, then there are clearly implications for the way in which we plan and organize the learning experience.

Surface learning	Deep learning
Intention to recall and reproduce lecture notes	Relating concepts to existing knowledge and understanding and to everyday life
Sole aim to pass assessments	Organizing and structuring new information
Passively accepting teacher's ideas or notes	An interest in understanding new materials
No reflection	Challenging new concepts and reading widely
No concept of overall patterns or themes	Examining the logic of the development
Treating assignments as a burden	Determining what is significant

Figure 4.4 The characteristics of deep and surface learning (as summarized by Reece and Walker 2007: 54–6)

Graham Gibbs himself suggested a range of teaching strategies and methods which can foster deep learning including: independent learning, problem-based learning, reflection, group work, learning by doing and project work (Gibbs 1992, cited in Harkin et al. 2001: 49). Some of these we shall revisit in more detail later.

Unfortunately, all too often, even with activities that appear to be designed to encourage a deep, investigative approach such as research assignments, 'students today commonly adopt surface learning. This is an understandable response to a teaching environment which fails to encourage them to adopt a deep approach' (Race and Pickford 2007: 22) That is, rather than developing their own strategies to solve problems set by the teacher, they will seek ways to come up with the 'right answer' in some cases aided by the teacher who might create a formula or task book to ensure that they do. In an environment where institutions, colleges and schools, are judged by results, this is a very tempting option.

You can find out more about these 'theories of learning' from any text on learning and teaching such as Armitage et al.'s (2007) *Teaching and Training in Post-Compulsory Education*, Capel et al.'s (2009) *Learning to Teach in the Secondary School* and Geff Petty's (2004) *Teaching Today: A Practical Guide*.

How can we make learning more effective?

So what have we learnt about effective learning from the above? Different theorists have had different ideas about this, but if we are to engage our learners in activities that will lead to meaningful learning experiences and, therefore, deep learning that will have a lasting value, it would seem that they need to be active rather than passive learners. As we have seen, the travel and tourism curriculum offers unique opportunities for developing such learning environments, so we can consider two theories that have been particularly influential during the twentieth century.

Experiential learning

We have seen that to stimulate 'deep learning' the learner must be actively engaged in the process of learning. It would seem to be obvious that, central to this approach, is the experience that the learner brings to the dialogue.

One of the most influential educationalists of the twentieth century was undoubtedly John Dewey. As an acknowledged pragmatist and political philosopher, his argument was that: 'learning rests on a mode of life where reason is exercised through problem solving, where the individual participates and contributes to the collective good of society and in the process constitutes their own development' (Olson, cited in Fegas and Nicoll 2008: 44). Thus, his views on the value and continuity of experience have informed a number of others who have developed this notion of 'experiential learning'. Kolb (1984), building on the work of Kurt Lewin, developed a model based on Dewey's proposition of internal and external experience, which has provided the basis for the planning of programmes adopting experiential learning methods. We have already looked at Kolb's model in relation to Honey and Mumford's learning styles (see Figure 4.2). The model is cyclical, meaning that each phase leads to the next and the learning is, therefore, a continuous process. The learner begins with knowledge and experience already gained (concrete experience) and, after reflection and experimentation with new ideas, leads to further experience. How does this work in practice?

> **Reflection 4.4**
>
> In a lesson on customer service, we want our learners to evaluate the learner's effectiveness of dealing with disruptive customers.
>
> Using the experiential learning cycle, how might you approach this lesson?
>
> What would be the benefits of experiential learning in this case?

Social learning

It might be noted that Olson's view on Dewey's proposition implies that meaningful learning takes place in a social context. Again, this is a theme that has been taken up and developed by others: Bandura (1969) and Vygotsky (d.1936) saw that while learners brought their own wealth of 'internal knowledge' to the learning environment, this would be developed by others more knowledgeable, those with knowledge 'external' to the learner, such as the teacher or even learner-peers. This element of development through shared knowledge Vygotsky described as the zone of proximal development (1962) and Bandura developed a theory of social learning where people learn chiefly through social interaction and the sharing of knowledge and experience.

So what are the implications for us as teachers of travel and tourism? Surely this means that learning is not something that happens in isolation, but that it happens through shared experiences. Strategies that enable this sharing of experience, then, will perhaps contribute towards more effective learning.

Developing expert learners through facilitative approaches

The experts are very good at telling us how they think learning takes place and, to be fair, most of them have worked experimentally to test out their theories. Dewey, for example, set up an experimental school at the University of Chicago where he developed practices that have influenced teaching throughout the twentieth century and now beyond, opening up his classrooms to create social learning spaces where learners might engage in cooperative, investigative, experiential learning involving projects that crossed subject boundaries.

What kinds of strategies and methods can we employ to develop not only our learners' knowledge of travel and tourism but also their capacity to learn? We have seen that there does seem to be a general consensus that to be truly effective inter-active, experiential learning approaches are important. So what kinds of specific approaches are available to us?

Susan Wallace (2005) distinguishes between strategies and methods, and this would seem to be helpful. Strategies generally refer to an overall approach to an activity such as whether the class would engage in group work or individual research and study, or whether they would work together as a whole class. The methods would refer to the learning activity itself. For example, the class might be divided into small groups (a strategy) to prepare for a role play or to research a topic for presentation (methods). On the other hand, the topic might be one that would benefit from whole-class engagement (a strategy) in a discussion (a method). The strategy, then, refers to the organization of the activity, whereas the method describes how the learners will engage in learning within that strategy.

Reflection 4.5

If a group visit to a local tourist attraction is a teaching strategy, what learning *methods* might you employ to ensure that the learners made the most of the opportunity?

It would be helpful, of course, to first define what the purpose of the visit is.

The choice of strategies and methods, as we have seen, will depend on the topic to be studied and possibly the level, but, almost certainly, the nature of the group, relationships within the group, their prior experiences and their preferred way of learning. For example, not all groups by any means will willingly engage in role-play activities.

Briefly, here are some methods employing experiential and interactive, social learning strategies that you might use to develop effective learning.

Some learning activities (methods)

Discussion

As an introduction to a lesson, discussion can be an indispensable way of immediately engaging learners interactively, perhaps finding out what they already know about a new topic or recalling one which you are continuing from a previous session. It is also invaluable in encouraging learners to share their experiences and to develop their own opinions.

Simulation, role play, games and case studies

These are all methods that appear to be very similar and may often be confused but, basically, they are ways in which learners can engage interactively through creating realistic, experiential situations in the classroom. David Jaques and Gilly Salmon in their comprehensive text *Learning in Groups* give the following accounts.

'*Simulations* are working representations of reality. [They are set in] a specific context or scenario . . . They allow students to explore social or physical systems where the real things are too expensive, complex, dangerous, fast or slow for teaching purposes' (Jaques and Salmon 2007: 140). An example of this would be dealing with a person having an asthma attack on an airplane. Clearly, one would hope that they might never have to actually experience this, but they must be prepared.

'*Role Play* involves people imagining that they are either themselves or someone else in a particular situation. They are asked to behave as they feel that person would, and to try behaviours that may not normally be a part of their repertoire' (Jaques and Salmon 2007: 141).

Reflection 4.6

Consider the role-play scenario in Figure 4.5.

How would you manage this in your lesson?

What problems can you foresee?

How would you improve it?

'*Games* (are) group exercises in which players cooperate or compete towards a given end within a regime of specific rules. Players behave as themselves' (Jaques and Salmon 2007: 140). Two groups of students studying community development, for example, might be given the task to design a holiday activity programme for 9- to 11-year-old children which is offered, in competition with each other, for tender to a local authority. The outcome could be decided from presentations to a selected panel of experts.

'*Case studies* are descriptions of a possible real-life event presented in order to illustrate special and/or general characteristics of a problem' (Jaques and Salmon 2007: 140). Given the role play in Figure 4.5 as a case study, students could be asked discuss possible solutions to the problem without actually acting it out.

Clearly, the case study could form the basis of role-play scenario, and elements of the game example are either a simulation or role play. As Jaques and Salmon (2007: 140) point out, 'All of these definitions are a matter of degree and balance – combinations abound.' The differences are probably not too important, but as ways of experiencing the realities of working environments in different ways to different degrees they are invaluable. However, as always it is of utmost importance that the exercise should be contextualized in the learning environment through careful preparation and followed by debrief and feedback. In fact, some role-play events can become very fraught and passions can run high as learners get into role: on such occasions the debrief is most necessary to bring the learners back to their reality.

The scenario takes place in a Spanish resort hotel.

A child has fallen from apparatus while playing in the supervised crèche and has suffered an injury which requires a visit to the local doctor's surgery.

The parents must be contacted and informed of the incident without causing them undue alarm.

Characters in the role play will be the crèche supervisor, the resort representative and one of the parents.

Figure 4.5 Role-play scenario

Applied learning

The term applied learning is widely used now to describe activities that relate directly to occupational roles. Most of the above will provide opportunities to develop such activities but, of course, much learning in the travel and tourism curriculum is best experienced through practical activity either directly in the workplace or through simulation or role play. The NVQ for travel services, for example, would be meaningless unless the learner could actually practise selling holidays with a group of their peers.

Making the most of educational visits and work placements

Of course, there is nothing quite like experiencing the real working environment to capture the full flavour of the travel and tourism industry. Visits to tourism venues, for example, preferably supported by a talk and/or a guided tour by an expert practitioner with time for questions, will be invaluable in placing the theoretical activities of the classroom into the context of the realities of the workplace. However, such visits will require in-depth planning to prepare learners for the experience so that they can make the most of it. Worksheets and questionnaires will help to focus their enquiries on relevant information. Trawling the Internet will give them an insight, and group discussion may help to refine their research. Subsequently, the visit should be followed up perhaps with an assignment and/or group presentations in order, again, to consolidate learning. Examples of these activities can be found in Chapters 5 and 6 where we consider assessment methods such as assignments and resources that include the workplace.

Work placements do, of course, give learners first-hand experience of working in the industry. However, again, this should not be regarded as a one-off experience unrelated to classroom activity. There should be careful preparation through discussion and research prior to the experience so that learners have some idea of what to expect, with research to carry out while in placement, identifying important aspects of the industry and its working practices. Worksheets might be appropriate, but perhaps a journal with daily activities might be more useful.

The role of formative assessment in facilitating learning

Although we shall discuss assessment in Chapter 5, it is appropriate to briefly raise the issue of formative assessment at this point, for this is the ongoing assessment throughout the learning experience where the learner can identify what progress they have made, what still needs to be done and in which direction to take their learning next.

Preparing for effective learning in the travel and tourism lesson

Having considered the various factors that can stimulate and affect learning and strategies and methods, we now need to consider what this all means when confronted by a class of eager (or perhaps even not so eager!) learners. After all, ensuring that our learners are actually benefiting from our lessons must be a major concern for the dedicated teacher.

Preparing the learning environment

One of the first things we need to consider is the, often neglected, learning environment. Abraham Maslow in his seminal and very well-known work on the 'hierarchy of needs' would say that, unless the environment is comfortable (both physically and psychologically) and stimulating, very little learning could take place. Although his work was aimed at business and industrial environments, Figure 4.6 shows how his ideas might be interpreted for the classroom.

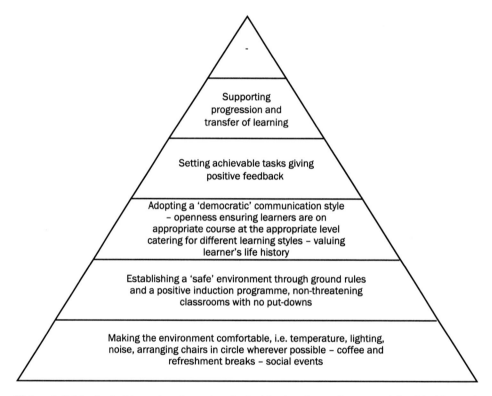

Figure 4.6 Maslow's hierarchy of needs adapted for teachers of young adults (Harkin et al. 2001: 62)

Even the layout of the desks or working spaces in a classroom can make a statement about the teacher's intentions and have a major impact on the learners' expectations as they enter the room.

Reflection 4.7

What kind of teaching activity would rows of desks suggest to you? Conversely, what about the horseshoe layout or blocks of three or four tables forming a wider working space?

But we make assumptions about each of these layouts. If we recall the discussion on learning styles it is possible that some students may feel that they respond better to the 'lecture room' layout, and for a university lecture in a tiered lecture hall with perhaps 60 or more students what alternatives are there?

The rationale for the horseshoe layout is that it brings the teacher closer to the learners enabling better eye contact and helps to include everyone into the group. However, discussion with some adult learners revealed that they felt 'exposed' and psychologically uncomfortable in this arrangement and preferred a layout where they could sit behind other people. How many of us, given the option, sit in the front row at a lecture?

Working around grouped tables, however, suggests interactive learning and presents the opportunity for small group work, although it can present problems where the focus of the session needs to be centralized, perhaps focused on the teacher.

As we have already suggested, such issues are not set in stone but will be determined by the nature of the group, their preferred way of learning and, perhaps, the subject and the context.

There are, of course, a number of things that we can also do to 'set the scene' and create an environment that focuses the learners on travel and tourism in order to stimulate learning. The following is an extract from an observation report on a lesson, the aim of which was 'To explore Greece as a holiday destination'. It was observed by two people assessing a trainee on teaching practice:

> As the assessors climbed up the dingy stairs (towards the classroom) they began to hear Greek music coming from the classroom: this was an audio-cassette provided by the class teacher.
>
> Inside the classroom walls and part of the whiteboard contained bright colourful posters obtained by the teacher from the Greek Tourist Board. The teacher herself was even dressed in Greek national colours . . .
>
> (Greenwich University)

Although the classroom was situated in 'an industrial part of town on the third floor (no lift!) in an old converted warehouse', clearly the teacher had thought carefully about how to bring Greece to life for her students despite the ambient environment.

Reflection 4.8

How might you prepare a stimulating learning environment for one of the following lessons?

1   A study of local heritage sites.
2   Organizing a children's activity day in a Spanish holiday resort.
3   In-flight customer service.

What does the travel and tourism lesson plan look like?

In Chapter 2 we looked at the scheme of work as the mid- to long-term planning process of our curriculum and briefly discussed the role of the lesson plan as the preparation for putting the scheme into action.

Good planning is essential if we are to make the most of the time we have with our students and ensure that the learning is effective.

A well-designed lesson plan will:

- make clear exactly what it is you want your students to learn;
- structure activities that will enable them to achieve this bearing in mind the opportunities that the topic provides to stimulate learning and also the profiles of the learners as discussed previously in this chapter;
- identify ways that you can assess whether they are achieving your lesson aims both throughout the lesson and at the end;
- show how learning might be stimulated and supported by the use of appropriate resources.

The plan will also provide a good point of reference throughout the lesson to ensure that you are working within the given time frame and towards your proposed objectives.

Surely the committed teacher must begin by asking themselves several important questions. The first must be to clearly identify what they want their students to learn from the experience and why this is important: this would be the aim of the lesson. Having established this, they should ask how they would know that they had achieved this aim: this will help to identify not only the lesson objectives but also ways that learning activities should be organized in order to achieve them and how to assess whether they had or not. Finally, they should consider what resources would help them to achieve the aim.

Concerned that university students generally seemed to engage in surface learning (just sufficient to pass examinations and gain a degree), John Biggs (2007) analysed the learning situation and presented it in a way that he termed 'constructive alignment'.

Figure 4.7 is an adaptation of his more sophisticated model but shows clearly how learning, which is central to all our activities here, is first predefined by our objectives or what it is that we would like our learners to learn, and that meaning is constructed through the arrangement of 'appropriate learning activities'. This leads us back to the question of how we would know just what the learners take away from the experience.

The process of planning, therefore, begins with asking by identifying what the lesson is all about: the aim. In the case of the lesson plan in Figure 4.8 the aims are expressed in very general terms but identify that they are to, '[explore a] new criteria: the distribution channels and promotions used by tour operators'. Although this may seem to be rather general, this is the nature of an aim. As Geoff Petty (2004: 392) observes: 'Aims are like compass directions, indicating the general direction in which the teacher wishes to travel.' These are often taken from the awarding body

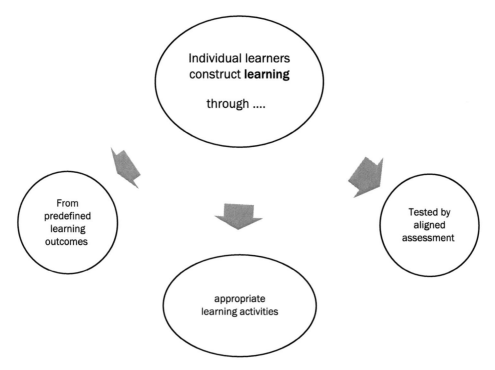

Figure 4.7 Constructive alignment model

 THE BLACKPOOL
Sixth Form College

Tutor: Zoe Slater	Subject & Level: Level 3, BTEC National Diploma Travel and Tourism	Group: A21ttd1350809
Date: 11/05/09	Session: 6	Room: W116

On Register:	Male: 7	Female: 8		

Main Aims of the Lesson:
This lesson is a continuation of the P3 criteria for unit 12: Tour operations. The learners are exploring a new area of the criteria: the distribution channels and promotions used by tour operators.

Learning Outcomes: *What should students be able to do?*
1) **Identify** the different distribution channels used by a tour operator.
2) **Determine** which distribution channel they prefer and **explain** why.
3) **Research** into the different distribution channel **to find** examples to use in their assessment work.
4) **Describe** the different promotional activities used by tour operators and **explain** their importance.

Directed Study Tasks (Homework) Set: *Tasks set for completion outside of lesson time.*
Previous Directed Study: Students have already had 2 lessons today, so there is no previous directed study for this lesson.

Directed Study from this lesson: To research into the term reservation team and to give examples of companies that use a reservation team (Pass 2 examples, Merit 3 examples, and Distinction 4 examples) and why?

Homework: To finish typing up the content of the lesson for submission Monday 18th May.

E-Learning / ILT:
Students are to use the Internet for research into examples of distribution and promotion to be used in their assignments. They will further use laptops to type up their assessment work (also used in their homework). Youtube clip is used in plenary. Finally there is a Powerpoint presentation to support the content of the lesson.

Differentiation and Stretch: *Include reference to the organisation of any group work*
Students will be **differentiated by outcome** in relation to the outcome of the paragraph generated for their assessment work. **Differentiation** will occur from the directed study task where students will be given a certain number of points that they need to have thought of which will be based on their progress grade, yet will be encouraged to **stretch** and exceed their MTG. Differentiation will occur from the starter activity like the directed study task by giving a certain number of distribution channels and promotional activities according to their progress grade. **Stretch** will also be used when asking learners to explain their answers and reasoning therefore, **differentiation via questioning** will occur, with more able students being asked to contribute answers to more complex questions. **Differentiation** will occur in the group work where the groups will be based on mixed ability in order to support and encourage all learners. Learners will further be **stretched and supported** in the individual time when students are completing the task and teacher is to check learning.

Resources used:
Laptops for write up of task.
Internet for research of suitable attraction
Promethean Board/Powerpoint
A3 paper/pens

Every Child Matters	Key Skills / LLN
~Enjoy & Achieve Students will work both independently & in small groups **(enjoy)** to complete tasks set, resulting in knowledge gained **(achieve)** **Enjoyment** can also emerge from the class debate which students tend to enjoy **~Positive Contribution** group tasks, ensuring all contribute and feedback allows all learners to **achieve**.	– Group work helps develop learners ability to **work with others** – Debate, group work and feeding back to the rest of the group contributes to developing **communication** skills. – Research into finding examples to support their assessment work help develop **ILT** skills along with typing up their assignment work. – **Problem solving skills** are touched upon when examining how tour operators can keep their spending on distribution to a minimum. – **Literacy/Language** is developed from learners working on their assessment work. – **Numeracy** skills will be encouraged through timed activities.

Time	Tutor Input	Student Activities: *What students are doing, how they are being organised*	Assessment of learning during the lesson
2 mins	**Introduction to the topic** – Tutor will display and discuss the topic objectives	**WHAT – WE are here to** – Students will take down key details of the session, to include objectives and proposed outcomes	
5 mins	What distribution channels can you think of?	Students to list the distribution channels they can think of that a tour operator uses. **Differentiated** by the number of examples given according to progress grade. Students to compile class list on board for all learners to take and use in assignment. (**Hint**: TA, online travel agents, direct – internet, tv, telesales, brochures, with newspapers)	**List** generated shows knowledge of distribution channels

5 mins	What is the purpose of Distribution? What distribution channel do you think is their preferred? Why?	Students to answer question. **Stretch** to establish what the TO must consider (cost, market it reaches) Students then independently answer question. **Stretch** for higher grade on explaining why they think that?	**Answers given** and **justification**
8 mins	Research into the distribution channels used by Thomas Cook	Students to research into the different methods that they can book a Thomas Cook holiday. (Thomas Cook direct, Online, holiday hypermarkets, TV, Travel agents – integrated and independent) **Stretch** classify into traditional and direct and state why they benefit from having a wide variety.	**List of distribution channels**
10 mins	**Debate** traditional methods v direct.	Group work on arguing their specified method. Students will need prompting to not only look at the advantages of their method but also the disadvantages of the other method. (Think of ABTA, AITO)	**Group discussions**
8 mins	Prompt in debate	Conduct Debate (learners to take notes during)	**Discussion in debate**
5 mins	**2nd part of lesson: Sales Promotion.** What is sales promotion and what is it purpose?	Students to independently write answer for the question and to discuss as a group.	Answers written down
12 mins	Hint: Students will need prompting on timing to move on to next questions.	Students to work in pairs to answer the questions on the powerpoint, before joining with another pair **(here higher and lower MTG mix)** to discuss answers. Teacher support according to MTG.	**Ideas** given pair and in group discussion.
5 mins	**Plenary** http://www. youtube.com/watch?v= HnPmUWNOd_w	Feedback to the rest of the group to develop their answers/notes.	**Answers given** in discussion.
5 mins	Question on other content of the lesson i.e what other distribution channel could they use?	Students to watch clip and discuss ideas on how sales promotions and distribution channels work together.	Ideas given.
5 mins	**Directed Study** – To research into the term reservation team and to give examples of companies that use a reservation team (Pass 2 examples, Merit 3 examples, and Distinction 4 examples) and why? **Homework**: Continue with write up for submission Monday 18th.		

Evaluation:

Figure 4.8 Exemplar lesson plan

specifications and are a guide as to the detail of the objectives, or intended learning outcomes, which are the means by which we can arrive at the destination or aim. The objectives are how we identify what exactly the learners should have learnt by the end of the lesson. In fact that very phrase is often used on lesson plans and you should be able to answer the question, 'What should the learners be able to do?' In the case of our example, '**Identify** the different distribution channels used by a tour operator. **Determine** which distribution channel they prefer and why' would be two such examples.

So, if our lesson is to be 'constructively aligned' we next need to decide upon the learning activities that will enable the learners to achieve the objectives and then, finally, to devise ways of determining how we will know that they have achieved them. This is the subject of Chapter 5, but at this stage we need to note that assessment is integral to the whole learning process.

Reflection 4.9

We have considered how the aims and objectives have determined the structure of the lesson in Figure 4.8, now carry this analysis a step further and consider the following:

- The sequencing and variety of the activities
- Assessment of learning both throughout the lesson and at the end
- Resources
- Identification of opportunities to develop key/functional skills (Chapter 3)
- Identification of opportunities to achieve PLTS (Chapter 3)
- Planning for differentiated and personalized learning

Summary

This chapter has been all about the front-line experience of learning and teaching. Whatever the background of the subject and the theories about curriculum, interacting with the learners in the classroom is the ultimate aim of our studies here. So we have tried to understand first, what our travel and tourism learners are likely to want out of the experience: their expectations. If we can analyse that, then perhaps we can identify the best way to teach them.

To help us with this task we have considered a range of theories about what it means to learn something and about how people learn. Our quest has been to try to identify how we create effective learning environments specific to the travel and tourism curriculum. The conclusions we hope you will have reached are based on the nature of the subject. The premise on which it is based is, after all, that it is concerned with human physical activity, so active, experiential, applied learning is going to be a major strategy for the teacher of travel and tourism.

However, we must not forget that, like most disciplines, this activity is supported by a great deal of academic, theoretical study and that all of our learners will benefit from a deeper understanding of the subject that studies bring at their respective levels. Indeed some will want to study this theory in great depth. Our challenge, then, is how to make this meaningful and interesting. I hope that we have addressed this sufficiently for you to be able to develop your own creative strategies which will engage your learners and motivate them in their studies.

Finally, we looked at how you can organize this learning experience in the most effective way and have used the model of 'constructive alignment' as a guide. You can look this up in more detail in John Biggs's (2007) *Teaching for Quality Learning at University* but it is important to note the role that assessment plays in the model, and this is the subject of the next chapter.

5

Assessing the travel and tourism curriculum

In this chapter we will be looking at:

- what we mean by 'assessment'
- the reasons why we assess
- different types of assessment
- the ways that different travel and tourism programmes are assessed
- the principles of assessment applied to the travel and tourism curriculum
- different methods of assessment used in the travel and tourism curriculum
- how to plan an assessment strategy
- how to design assessments for travel and tourism.

Introduction

So that we are all clear about what this chapter is really about, it might be pertinent to ask the question, 'What is assessment?' In educational circles, it generally means finding out what learners know or can do, and what they have learnt. Armitage and Renwick (2008: 5) would say that it is 'about the judgements of assessors with relation to the quality of student achievement'. The 'assessors', of course, could be any number of people from awarding body examiners, to you, the teacher, or even the learners themselves, as in peer- and self-assessment.

Reflection 5.1

Think back to the last two or three times that you were assessed for anything – an examination for a degree, or even a driving test. How many different ways can you remember being assessed? Were they accurate tests of what you had learnt?

In Chapter 4, we showed how assessment must be seen as an important component of the learning process and not as something just tacked onto the end of a course as a measure of whether or not the learner has 'passed' or 'failed'. It is through testing ourselves against what we set out to learn (our intended outcomes) that we can determine whether or not we have, indeed, learnt whatever it was and what perhaps still needs to be learnt. So that check on learning, the assessment, is an important aspect of the learning process, without it and the feedback that confirms what learning has taken place, it is doubtful that we will know that we have learnt anything at all. It is important to acknowledge that by 'feedback' we mean not only the comments on a test paper, but also that which results from self-reflection.

So assessment and the feedback that is integral to it are essential to the learning process. Assessment should not be the main objective of your learning programmes, though frequently it is. We would then say that the learning is 'assessment driven', and this would tend to lead to 'surface learning' when the learner only aims to acquire sufficient knowledge to pass the assessment rather than to learn for learning's sake.

Assessment should support and, indeed, enhance learning. Whether it comes at the end of your programmes or at intervals during them, it offers a form of feedback in answer to the question, 'How am I doing?' Such assessment is 'formative' assessment for learning because it supports the development and growth of the learner. By answering this question, we will know whether or not the learner has 'got it' (that is the knowledge and understanding) and see what needs to be done to help them 'get it'. Assessment that comes as an end test is called 'summative' because it is a test of the sum total of the learner's knowledge and understanding.

In this chapter we look at different forms of assessment used in travel and tourism programmes and this might be a good point at which to refer back to Figure 2.1. Morrison and Ridley's matrix shows how different ideologies generate different assessment methodologies, and we can relate this to our various travel and tourism programmes. A level, for example, arguably follows the classical humanist, elitist, knowledge-based curriculum and is assessed largely by examination, whereas the National Diploma has a more 'progressive humanist' agenda favouring coursework-based assessment which requires a formative approach as learners develop their knowledge and understanding through autonomous learning activities. On the other hand, many assessments in travel and tourism are outcome driven and instrumentalist, such as an NVQ in Preparing an Itinerary for a Business Customer, in which learners have to prove competence by performing the task successfully.

The merits and appropriateness of each type of assessment will be considered in terms of the principles of validity, authenticity, reliability and practicability, and we further examine the methods that each employs, with suggestions as to how to design assessment activities that fulfil these criteria.

Finally, we look at how you can design your own assignments for coursework and, in the light of the above, we need to consider the following:

- what constitutes success and how you measure it.
- how this 'journey' is staged in terms of achievement, in a way that is realistic to a learner and acceptable to a curriculum.
- how you convey this information to your learners.

Why do we need to assess our learners?

Reflection 5.2

Referring back to the assessments you identified in Reflection 5.1, why were you assessed? What did the assessment tell you about 'the quality of your achievement'?

Now think about the last time you assessed a group of travel and tourism learners, and ask the same questions:

- Why did you assess them?
- What did the assessment tell you about the 'quality of their learning'?

Assessment, then, is how we measure what our learners know and can do or what they have learnt. But why do we need to know this? The following are some good reasons for assessing them.

We find out what the learners already know and can do

As a teacher it is helpful to know what our learners know before they begin a programme of learning so that we can adapt the plan accordingly: a test which does this would be called 'diagnostic'. This is an essential form of assessment if we are to design 'personalized learning' programmes.

We find out what they have learnt from our lessons

Clearly, this is important information for us to ascertain whether or not our planned teaching has been effective and if it is necessary to modify our plans. It also serves as a reminder to the learners of what the lesson was all about.

Having found out what our students have learnt, this information is used in a number of ways:

We can evaluate our learning programmes

There are a number of indicators that we can use to measure the success of our programmes, but assessing the outcomes in terms of the quality of student learning is probably the most obvious way.

We can monitor learner progress

Assessment provides a check on what has been learnt and what still needs to be done: which of our learners has 'got it' and which ones need further attention. In this sense, with quality feedback, it becomes 'formative'. It will also tell us whether any of them are ready to progress to higher levels such as HNDs or Foundation Degrees.

Assessment can motivate our learners

Knowing that there is a deadline for an assignment or that there is a test or examination coming up is a sure way of motivating learners but, even more important, is the inspiration they get from any successful assessment.

Assessment provides a public record of the efficacy of the programme

Naturally any education system needs to measure success and the success or otherwise of educational establishments and training providers is continually measured in terms of results and grade scales to establish their position in the league tables. This approach has tended to lead to a qualification-driven environment which perhaps overlooks to some extent the benefits to the individual learner and the values that accrue from the learning process itself.

How is travel and tourism assessed?

We have seen how different kinds of knowledge can be tested or assessed, in different ways. The discussion and debates generated by issues such as sustainable tourism and the impact of 9/11 are probably best examined through essay-type assessments, such as might be found in A levels, and Foundation Degrees. Research-based learning which has formed the basis of BTEC National Diplomas for a good many years now, is assessed through assignments, and practical skills tests, dealing with customer complaints perhaps, or booking a holiday, should be seen to be achieved through the actual performance of the task.

However, whatever the form of assessment, we need to determine the standards against which we will measure success.

> **Reflection 5.3**
>
> Consider three different assessments that you have conducted as a teacher of travel and tourism and try to identify how success was measured.
>
> - Was the test appropriate to the knowledge required?
> - Was it against a set standard, or against a hypothetical 'average mark'?
> - What did this tell you about your progress (or your learners' progress)?

Deciding on the standards: referencing

'Referencing' provides us with a framework for designing our programmes because it defines the standard, or reference, against which we measure achievement.

Criterion referencing

The measure here is a criterion: a standard is set, generally by an awarding body, and success is measured by achievement of that standard with no reference to how many learners achieve it. A number of programmes in travel and tourism are criterion referenced, such as NVQs and National Diplomas.

Figure 5.1 is an example of an element from an NVQ in Travel Services identifying specific assessment criteria which the learner must clearly demonstrate before achieving the award. Figure 5.2, on the other hand, shows part of a grading grid for a National Diploma programme in Travel and Tourism, again with clear criteria for assessment.

The difference to note here is that, whereas the NVQ criteria are simply achieved, or not, by demonstration, the National Diploma criteria allow for different standards

---

Unit 204 (T19) Help Customers to choose and Book Travel Services

What you must do: To meet the National Standards you must

1. Help customers to identify and select their travel requirements by
a. Greeting your customers in a prompt, friendly and confident way
b. Clarifying your customer's **travel services** requirements using suitable **questioning techniques** and listening skills and recording the results
c. Questioning your customer on their travel requirements and taking opportunities to offer any **additional services**
d. Summarising your understanding of your customer's needs accurately
e. Accurately calculating and advising your customers of the total cost of their travel requirements

2. Complete travel services bookings by
a. Confirming bookings for **travel services** and any **additional services** that accurately match the details agreed with your customer
b. B. completing the booking to meet your organisation's procedures and legal requirements
c. Processing all booking administration promptly, correctly and following your organisation's procedures
d. Storing booking information and documentation securely following your organisation's procedures and legal requirements

3. Process post-booking documentation by
a. Ensuring bookings have a supplier confirmation that matches the services booked
b. Issuing the correct copies of booking documents to the relevant person(s)
c. Updating booking documentation promptly and accurately when required
d. Referring all matters outside your work responsibilities or experience to the relevant person

4. Receive, prepare and issue travel documentation by
a. Ensuring all documentation received matches the travel services booked
b. Taking prompt and suitable action to resolve any documentation discrepancies before issue to customers
c. Issuing complete and accurately assembled documentation and tickets to your customers within the required time scale and following your organisation's procedures
d. Clearly reconfirming the booking details to your customer
e. Explaining all travel arrangements clearly and fully to your customer in a way that they will understand
f. Ensuring your customer has fully understood their travel arrangements and is satisfied with your service before they leave your premises
g. Competing all customer records fully and accurately and passing them to the relevant person(s) promptly

Figure 5.1 An NVQ element of assessment (https//www.cityandguilds.com/documents/ind_travel/SP-02-4847.pdf)

Grading Criteria

To achieve a **pass grade** the evidence must show that the learner is able to:	To achieve a **merit grade** the evidence must show that, in addition to the pass criteria, the learner is able to:	To achieve a **distinction grade** the evidence must show that, in addition to the pass and merit criteria, the learner is able to:
P1 Describe (giving examples including domestic, inbound and outbound tourism) the components of the travel and tourism industry	M1 Explain how the components of travel and tourism interrelate, giving examples that include domestic, inbound and outbound tourism	D1 Assess how the roles and responsibilities of travel and tourism organisations from the profit and not for profit sectors affect their operations
P2 Describe the ways that components of travel and tourism interrelate	M2 Compare the role and responsibilities of travel and tourism organisations from the profit and not for profit sectors	D2 Recommend how the travel and tourism industry could respond to key trends and factors affecting the future development of travel and tourism
P3 Describe the roles and responsibilities of travel and tourism organisations from the profit and not for profit sectors	M3 Explain how recent developments have shaped the present day travel and tourism industry and how key trends and factors are likely to shape the industry in the future	
P4 Describe four recent developments (from the 1960s onwards) that have shaped the present day travel and tourism industry		
P5 Describe three key trends and three factors that are affecting or are likely to affect the development of travel and tourism		

Figure 5.2 National Diploma grading chart (http//www.edexcel.com/migrationdocuments/ BTEC%20Nationals/315894_BN018369_NACD_in_Travel_and_Tourism_L3_Issue_2.pdf)

of achievement. This is one of the major areas of debate in the competency assessed curriculum, that there is little motivation to excel in completing an NVQ that merely demands 'achievement'.

Vocational assessment is generally underpinned by the development of practical skills, for example, managing booking systems. Perhaps the best measure of this is assessment of these skills in the workplace, as part of a structured assessment experience for an NVQ programme. The learner, having been shown, may practice, reflect and, finally, be summatively assessed against the criteria.

Norm referencing
While a criterion approach may prove beneficial to the learner, the assessor and potentially the employer, a different approach may be required in considering an assessment protocol that would sufficiently engage a learner seeking to extend knowledge or a deeper understanding of the processes. Often such assessments use

examinations or tests in which learners are measured against each others' performance as in A level Travel and Tourism: this is known as 'norm' referencing because
it measures the success of learners against their peers and against what is considered
to be the average standard. So about 50 per cent may pass, and 50 per cent may not.

Ipsative assessment

Throughout this publication we have referred to personalized learning and the focus
on the development of each individual learner. Ipsative assessment is the way in which
we can measure this development because it is self-referenced, that is it measures an
individual's progress from one given point in time to another. In this case, a diagnostic
assessment is most important so that we have the measure of the learner's progress at
a particular point. When we assess them later, we can measure how much they have
improved against their own standard. This has been known as 'value-added' learning.

Ipsative assessment might be used alongside criterion referencing where the
learner sets out to achieve a standard and having achieved this can identify which
standard to work towards next. Although NVQs may be considered somewhat
behaviourist in design, they do also have some 'learner-centred' attributes which allow
the participant some measure of autonomy in deciding how best to achieve the award,
as the NVQ level 2 specifications for Teaching, Coaching and Instructing inform us:
'The candidate and assessor should discuss the best way of assessing each element in
this unit and plan how it will be done' (SPRITO 1997: 14).

Assessing different travel and tourism programmes

Types of summative assessment

So far we have discussed a number of issues concerning purposes and standards, and
you may have noticed that this has been contextualized by referring to different types
or modes of assessment: examinations, coursework and practical demonstration.
Before approaching the subject of planning a strategy and designing an assessment, it
would be helpful to consider the merits and problems of these modes in a little more
depth.

Examinations

Generally, as we have already suggested, examinations are norm-referenced forms of
assessment that tend to focus on the testing of knowledge: A levels and GCSE would
be a typical example. They are tests of knowledge acquired during the course of the
programme of learning. That is not to say that these qualifications do not include
coursework which may have an element of criterion referencing, but, ultimately, we
expect a certain percentage to pass and a certain percentage to fail.

Although coursework is a very popular form of assessment, there are many strong
arguments for the inclusion of an examination-based system to either partly or wholly
replace the coursework-led approach.

Generally examinations are more convenient to organize and manage; they can
be modified and take less time in terms of development and grading. Examination-
based systems can also provide more rigid external validity (see later) and elicit

population normative statistics which can form a point of reference or group comparison. In addition, achievement data are easily stored and potentially provide longitudinal comparative performance data.

The key arguments against an examination-based system in vocational learning are that often the greatest value of vocational programmes is the opportunity to provide consistent formative feedback as opposed to this clinical summative approach. Critics of this approach could also point to measurement of only shallow learning, and that criterion-based assessment is in fact more reliable than norm-referenced data, particularly for vocational areas such as travel and tourism where practical applications such as the ABTAC Travel Geography assessment, which is an open-book but time-bound assessment, provide evidence of the learner's competence.

Coursework

Coursework generally refers to assignments that are centre-devised measures of performance. It could be practical, theoretical, academic or vocational.

In most instances it is regulated or verified by an awarding body and exists in most travel and tourism programmes, including GCSEs, GCE A levels, BTEC level 2 and level 3 Diplomas and the 14–19 Diploma.

One of the characteristics of coursework assessment is that the summative assessment can be spread across the duration of the course. Consider a BTEC National or First in Travel and Tourism where centres design their own assessments. There is encouragement by the awarding body to spread the summative assessment throughout the length of the programme. Similarly NVQ travel programmes measure competence for a range of skills, such as customer service, which lend themselves to a range of assessment practices, with the focus of an eventual, refined product, for example, being able to competently deal with a customer complaint at a resort.

In a review of coursework, 'A review of GCE and GCSE coursework arrange-ments' (QCA 2005) there was an endorsement of this approach to assessment in terms of the benefit to learners, and of its general advantages which were seen to outstrip the potential shortcomings. It did, however, also raise some areas of concern.

It suggested that all assessors must authenticate the work of the learners that they assess, effectively providing a professional endorsement, especially where coursework was not completed in the centre. Many centres ask that the learner submitting the work authenticates their own submission, thereby helping to eliminate plagiarism. Attempting to claim the work of another as your own is nothing new, but temptation now exists in a number of different ways, from directly copying from web pages to purchasing coursework from organizations that will produce coursework on demand for a fee. Information technology and specialized software such as 'Turnitin' is now available that will identify plagiarized submissions.

Since 2007, all teachers and lecturers are required to register with the General Teaching Council (GTC) or the Institute for Learning (IfL) and evidence of mal-practice in this, or any other, matter could result in being effectively 'struck off'. In addition it is possible for awarding bodies to be disqualified from offering a set of qualifications.

However, perhaps the main advantage of coursework and a principal difference between this and examination-based assessment is that it focuses on the processes of learning as much as the content. The learner is expected to analyse the task set and interpret it so that they conduct research and present their findings in the form of the assignment. Throughout the duration of the programme there is a need for regular progress checks that will include feedback given to learners about their progress. Thus the assessment is, to an extent, also formative not only for the benefit of the learner but also the tutor who is in a position to make regular reviews of their own teaching.

Surprisingly, many learners who decide to follow a coursework-focused programme, often because they are disenchanted by the examination system which has failed them to date, find the process of continuous assessment much more onerous than they thought it would be.

Practical demonstration

Much of the travel and tourism curriculum, certainly up to and including level 3, has a practical focus. The industry is ultimately concerned with providing a service to the public, even if there are political, social and environmental issues to take into consideration. Thus, there will be opportunities to assess learners through practical demonstration. How else could you assess a learner's capabilities in dealing with customers' complaints or their efficiency in booking a holiday? The specifications for many programmes recommend that such knowledge and skills should only be assessed through practical demonstration.

In fact, many travel and tourism programmes now include elements of at least two and perhaps all three modes of assessment. A levels and GCSEs, we have already noted, have coursework as well as time-constrained examinations, and National Diplomas, traditionally assessed by coursework, now have timed-constrained assignments completed under examination conditions.

Such a system perhaps answers all the criticisms of each type of assessment. Provided that balance is maintained between them, it would ensure the opportunity for academic rigour through the examination, provide opportunities for learner-centred delivery and assessment through the coursework, and enable learners to be assessed on the merits of their practical performance. Perhaps this is only appropriate considering the cross-curricular nature of travel and tourism.

Reflection 5.4

Thinking about your own experiences of assessment again and comparing examinations, coursework and practical demonstration, which was your preferred option?

Does this depend on what was being assessed?

What were the benefits (and pitfalls) of each method in your experience?

Planning an assessment strategy

Planning for assessment is a vital part of an aligned approach to planning for learning, as we noted in Chapter 4. In an ideal situation it will involve a number of agencies, potentially including senior management, other teaching staff, industry stakeholders and employers and, wherever possible, the learners, who are more likely to achieve if they have a stake in their assessment design. A well-planned assessment strategy will identify areas of strengths and weakness and provide a challenging, vocationally relevant assessment plan.

To be meaningful and worthwhile, assessment measures should follow certain rules or principles. Here we visit the accepted principles and try to apply them to our design of travel and tourism assessments.

The principles of assessment applied to the travel and tourism curriculum

Validity

In short, validity is the fitness for purpose of an assessment tool. Does it accurately measure what it sets out to measure? Primarily this is the role of the awarding body who will seek to take measures to ensure this, either in the design of their own externally set assessments or in the moderation of internally centre-set assessment by a process of moderation or verification (see later in this chapter).

Tummons (2007: 38–9) suggests a differentiation in the types of validity:

Face validity is measured in the way in which an assessment looks like an assessment. In other words, it has academic credibility, is free from typographical or grammatical errors, and is possibly measured against existing or previous similar assessments. A well-written and functional assessment tool with an air of institutional formality is required to meet face validity.

Content validity is measured in terms of how the assessment tool matches the grading specification requirements and the clarity of assessment objectives. In other words, it will accurately reflect the content as set out in specifications and will not ask questions about material that is not included in them.

Construct validity will measure how closely the assessment assesses what the specification says it should measure. If the criterion requires that the learner is measured in terms of understanding and managing a booking system then a practical demonstration is a better way of testing them than asking them to write an essay about it in an examination. On the other hand, if we wanted to assess their specific knowledge of an overseas destination, then a more formal examination-based system may be more relevant.

Predictive validity is measured in terms of the degree to which predictions based on results can be used to determine future performance and achievement. Learners and providers are frequently asked not only to produce evidence of prior achievement, but also current predicted measures, such as a GCSE candidate who has applied to a local college for a level 3, National Diploma programme, or that same learner two years later who will be making an application to UCAS for an undergraduate degree.

Awarding bodies seek to establish validity by accrediting specifications with the approval of key government agencies such as the QCA. As we saw in Chapter 2, in 2010 all BTEC National and First programmes were reaccredited to embrace the Qualifications and Credit Framework and as a result significant alterations to the way in which the programmes are assessed have been made. As well as vocational updates, changes have been made to the names of the programmes, for example, BTEC travel and tourism programmes previously known as BTEC Nationals and Firsts have been retitled Level 3 Nationals and Level 2 Firsts respectively.

Assessment by awarding bodies of centre-designed assessments and indeed the quality of assessment decisions continues to be measured by a mixture of sampling methods, external quality assessment, moderation, verification and standardization.

Reliability

Assessment is considered reliable if, when applied on a number of occasions, the results produced are consistent. Rather than the focus on how appropriate an assessment tool is (validity), reliability is a measure of how consistent an assessment tool is, as well as its accuracy.

Reliability is measured by awarding bodies through examination or coursework standardization, methods for which will differ according to the assessment tools used.

An examination-led programme, such as A Level Travel and Tourism, ensures reliability through a system of rigorous standardization. Examiners mark a sample of work according to a set marking scheme which is, in turn, submitted for scrutiny at an Examiners' meeting, after which their work is carefully monitored by a lead examiner.

Standardization of coursework is achieved in standardization meetings in which moderators debate grade bands and score across a sample of submitted work, before embarking upon the responsibility of moderating assessed grades across a range of centre assessments.

Reflection 5.5

Consider the assignment set in Figure 5.3.

To what extent do think it fulfils the principles of validity?

Is it a valid test of the learner's ability to 'understand the retail and business travel environments; how advances in technology have affected retail and business travel operations and how retail travel organizations seek to gain competitive advantage'?

Can you think of ways that this might be assessed other than the report?

Would the report be a reliable test of the learner's understanding?

Note: The answer to the above may well be 'yes', and this is in no way to suggest criticism of the assignment. The exercise is intended to challenge you to consider your own alternatives.

THE BLACKPOOL
Sixth Form College

**Department of
Sport, Tourism & Health**

**National Diploma/Certificate in Travel and Tourism – Year 1
Unit 9 – Retail & Business Travel Operations**

Designed to cover:
    Learning outcome 1 – Understand the retail and business travel environments
    Learning outcome 2 – Understand how advances in technology have affected retail and business
    travel operations
    Learning outcome 3 – Understand how retail travel organizations seek to gain competitive
    advantage
Grading criteria – **P1-M1-D1 P2 P3-M2-D2**

Scenario:
You have a column in Travel Weekly and for the next edition of the trade paper; you have been asked to
prepare an article on the 'business and retail environment'.

Brief:
You must undertake research and prepare a **report** to outline the proposed content of the article.

Task 1 – P1 hand in 22ⁿᵈ March 2010

Describe the retail and business travel environment including the **relationship between retail and
business travel agents and other sectors of the travel and tourism industry**. Provide **examples** where
appropriate of different types of retail and business retailers **(P1)**, demonstrating a good understanding
of the types of agent available.
a) Describe the types of market **(Leisure and business)** each of the following types of agent attracts and
    the **products** and **services** each sell.

Describe supported by examples the following types of retail agents and their role
– **Independents**
– **Multiples**
– **Integrated**
– **E-agents**
– **Home workers**
– **Products and services – holidays and ancillary services**

Describe supported by examples the following types of business agents and their role
– **General business travel**
– **Corporate hospitality**
– **Incentive travel**
– **E-agent**
– **Products and services – scheduled flights, accommodation and ancillary sales.**

b) You are required to research and describe the legal and regulatory framework specific to the retail and
business travel sector including,
- **Trade Associations – ABTA**
- **Consortia e.g. Advantage Travel Centres**
- **Membership – International Air Transport Association (IATA)**
- **Licensing e.g. – Air Travel Organisers Licence (ATOL)**
- **The legal framework should include the EU Package Travel Regulations. The Financial Services
  Authority must also be described in relation to compulsory training for agents selling holiday
  insurance.**
Copyright: The Blackpool Sixth Form College

c) You will need to focus on the relationship between retail and business travel agents and other sectors of the travel and tourism industry.

The relationship must cover,
- **Integration (vertical & horizontal); agency agreements; commission levels; preferred operators; racking policies and financial bonding.**

Other sectors must include;
- **Accommodation, transport providers, ancillary providers e.g. car hire, insurance; tour operators.**

You must provide industry examples to help illustrate your understanding

Task 2a – M1 hand in 22nd March 2010
Using your knowledge from Task 1, **explain** how relationships operate in the retail and business travel environment and its impact on the travel industry as a whole **(M1)**.

You should make valid judgements with reasoned conclusions supported by industry examples such as the **impacts of differing commission levels on retail and business agents; the impact of dynamic packaging and the growth of low-cost scheduled airlines on the industry as a whole.**

Task 2b – D1 hand in 22nd March 2010
Provide a **general evaluation** but draw on examples from the industry, where they are appropriate and support points being made on the effectiveness of retail and business travel organisations and how they operate in the travel industry environment **(D1)**.

Your evaluation must be critical and show an understanding of both strengths and weaknesses in the industry. Areas to evaluate include,

- **The how up to date booking systems used compare to other types of organisations**
- **How responsive agencies are to meeting changing customer needs and expectations**
- **How effective commission levels are in raising agency sales.**

Task 3 – P2 hand in 22nd March 2010
a) Describe how technological advances have affected retail and business operations.
Technological advances include the **Internet as a method of distribution or a resource, advances in computer systems and transport e.g. Road, rail, air & sea changing reservation systems and methods of communication.**

b) Describe the **effect** each of these has on the operation of both the retail and business agent in terms of **sales (Volume systems & timing)** and **types of products** and **services sold** and **administration systems used**.

c) The effect on the operation must include distribution of the products and services offered to customers **e.g. via competition, integrated agents, direct sell.**

The **description must** also include the **effect on the booking process including the payment methods used and security systems required for credit card payments and computers**.

Task 4a – P3 hand in 22nd March 2010
a) Explain how retail travel organisations seek to gain a competitive advantage **(P3)**.

You must investigate different agents (multiple and independent) to determine the activities they undertake to gain competitive advantage over other retail agents or direct sell. Your explanation must include,
- **The level of service retail agents provides such as 'meet and greet' and appointment systems and how this gives the travel agent the competitive advantage.**
- **The level of staff training, for example selling skills and how this helps gain competitive advantage.**
- **Promotional activities e.g. discounting, low deposits, advertising and displays, explaining how these types of activities can give an agent edge over competition.**

Explain how the **range of products and services** offered, including **add-on-sales** and **ancillary products and services** can make a difference. You must also consider the activities **integrated agents** undertake to gain the edge over competition. For example retail agents **dynamic packaging** of holidays using low cost airlines. You must explain how these product innovations give a retail agent the competitive edge for example more **market share**.

Task 4b – M2 hand in 22nd March 2010
To successfully complete the article use the knowledge gained in P3 to compare the effectiveness of two retail travel organisations seeking to gain a competitive advantage **(M2)**.
The similarities and differences between the two will help you to explain how they impact on the effectiveness of the agents. Current and specific examples must be referred to.

Task 4c – D2 hand in 22nd March 2010
Recommend how the two retail travel agents can gain a competitive advantage by justifying points and providing evidence to support your suggestions. **(D2)**.

Figure 5.3 Exemplar assignment brief

Authenticity

Put simply, this is the suitability of the task. Consider the suitable forms of assessment available to an assessor for the delivery of an NVQ-type assessment in making an on-line booking where a written report would clearly not be suitable, and thus not authentic.

Grant Wiggins offers a definition of authenticity;

Engaging and worthy problems or questions of importance, in which students must use knowledge to fashion performances effectively and creatively. The tasks are either replicas of or analogous to the kinds of problems faced by adult citizens and consumers or professionals in the field.

(Wiggins 1993: 229).

There is no reason why, in this sense, the most authentic form of assessment is that which most mimics industry, and using the earlier example a practical assessment perhaps recorded may prove to be the most effective measure of assessment. In many cases it may be best to employ the planning backwards method (McDonald 1992). In this approach the assessor decides on the desired outcome of the test and the learner is then encouraged to demonstrate their mastery of the problem set. The assessor makes their judgement based on an established set of competencies set in an authentic assessment environment. Although this may provide a greater sense of authenticity as in, say work-based assessment of an NVQ, it does lead, as McDonald admits, to an assessment-led learning programme.

Practicability

Given the time available and the physical environment, is the assessment activity realistic? In some cases, it simply is not possible to arrange a totally authentic environment and we have to design a role play or case study. For example, although we may be able to organize educational visits abroad, we may not be able to arrange for our learners to experience the realities of being a resort representative and would need to rely on a role play or simulation to assess their competence in this role.

Differentiation

> Differentiation is . . . the process of identifying with each learner, the most effective strategies for achieving agreed targets.
>
> (Weston 1992: 21)

> Differentiation is about identifying and addressing the different needs, interests and abilities of all learners to give them the best possible chance of achieving their learning goals.
>
> (DfES 2004: 5)

In Chapter 4, we discussed the issues related to personalized learning and, as Brookfield (1998) observed, it can be very demanding if not impossible, to differentiate for every learner. However, we will no doubt be confronted with a class of individuals with different needs across the learning spectrum from very motivated and quick learners to those with special learning issues. As with all areas of teaching and learning, differentiation needs to be addressed within the assessment framework in order that each learner might be given every opportunity to demonstrate the quality of their learning. For example, all too often assessments contain what are described as extension activities, which in reality are just activities that provide the more able with something to do, rather than something which challenges them and stretches their analytical, comparative or evaluative skills.

The key to a successfully differentiated assessment activity is in the planning stage, in other words, you need to take into account prior and recent knowledge of your learners, in order that you may design activities that promote access to them all. Additional activities must be challenging and easily accessible. Increasingly it is necessary to establish personal targets and rely on good data from initial diagnostic assessment as well as reliable updates in documents such as Individual Learning Plans (ILPs) and learner passports to support assessment design.

Whatever the source, to ensure differentiation in travel and tourism assessment you must consider the following:

- practical ability
- maturity
- socio-economic status
- religious/cultural beliefs
- prior learning and knowledge including experience
- intrinsic motivation
- speed of learning
- specific individual need such as disability and language.

The traditional approach which focuses on the 'norm' is no longer acceptable and it is essential, given Brookfield's proviso mentioned in Chapter 3, and again in the spirit of Every Child (Learner) Matters, that we differentiate by outcomes as demonstrated by our assessment practices.

> **Reflection 5.6**
>
> To what extent has differentiation been embedded into the assignment in Figure 5.3?
>
> How would you improve this aspect of planning in this example?

Assessment design

Many travel and tourism programmes require the assessor to design the assessment material, and while this may be challenging, it should be considered an excellent opportunity to personalize assessment to suit a group of learners.

Consideration must be given to the following when planning assessment for a programme:

- the intended learning outcomes of the learning experience
- the grading criteria assuming a criterion-based system
- the most appropriate assessment tool (see next section)
- how feedback will be provided
- how and when summative feedback is managed.

As we noted in Chapter 4, following the principles of constructive alignment (Biggs 2007), the starting point will almost certainly be the learning outcomes or criteria which define what it is the learner is expected to achieve. The assessment design, therefore, will reflect how we can best create opportunities for the learner to demonstrate their achievement of the outcomes.

Earlier, when considering coursework, we looked at a unit from a National Diploma programme (Figure 2.9): the learning outcomes are clearly identified, so this would be the guide to your setting assessment tasks. However, although the outcomes are generally explicit and relate to the acquisition of knowledge, understanding and skills, it is possible that they might reflect formative, process- based criteria such as in Reflection 5.7.

> **Reflection 5.7**
>
> Although the following is taken from a specification for the Edexcel National Diploma in Sport, Impact and Sustainability in Outdoor Adventure (Unit 30, p. 287), the subject is appropriate for travel and tourism too.

'[The] grading criteria . . . require learners to plan, undertake and review a project based on the idea of environmental sustainability. . . . It is a really good opportunity for learners to be autonomous and independent.'

Could demonstrating 'autonomy and independence' in learning be considered an intended outcome? If so how would you grade this?

From the learner's point of view a clear assessment plan will enable them to engage more fully with the learning programme. In the spirit of autonomy, they will be able to organize their learning and integrate the assessment process into their own learning plan. It is also important to consider the impact of enabling learners' input in the design of their assessment and assisting them in recognizing their progress and achievement, thus developing a wider sense of responsibility for their own achievement in learning.

As previously mentioned, one of the challenges presented to new teachers on vocational programmes is the notion that they will be responsible for the design of assessment material. While this may at first appear to be daunting, when presented with a range of assessment tools and information about a group of learners many report this as a key strength of vocational courses.

Whichever tool is chosen for assessment we should ensure that we follow the principles of assessment discussed earlier, perhaps answering the following questions:

- Is the assessment a valid test of knowledge, understanding and skills? There should be no doubt what the assessment is measured against and where possible the criteria for assessment should be included. The task/s established to meet the criteria should be imaginative without ever deviating far from the assessment criteria.

- Is the assessment 'authentic'? Is it set in a realistic travel and tourism scenario which enables the learner to identify the purpose and context of the assessment? In a sense, this is a form of unsophisticated role play in which the learner may be asked to imagine a setting in which this assessment may be of value. A well-developed scenario can also influence career aims and extend an insight into a role that was not previously conceived.

- Does it differentiate appropriately? The assessment must be equitable and not exclude or disadvantage any member of any group to be assessed based on their gender, culture, disability, race or religious beliefs.

- Is it practicable? Assessment should be presented in such a way as to be easily accessed by the entire cohort. Increasingly there is a trend towards the use of technology in all aspects of teaching and learning. Assessment material previously presented in the form of a paper-based handbook may be more conveniently accessed electronically, for example via a web portal or virtual learning network, and while this may suit the needs of most, there may well be some without regular Internet access, and for whom the paper version remains the best option.

Assessment tools

Reflection 5.8

Think back over the last few courses that you have attended.

List at least ten different tests that you have done.

If you think that's too many turn to Figure 5.4 and see how many of your ideas are in that list.

Do you think that they were appropriate to what was being tested?

Written	Media based	Practical
Poster presentation/Leaflet presentation	Audio or video recording	Survey
	Website design	Project
Product evidence/artefact	Podcast	Field-based experiment
Work experience logbook	Post to forum (text, audio or video)	Role play
Presentation		Case studies
Work-based assessment	Recorded discussion	Witness statements or observation records
Portfolio of evidence	Annotated photographs	Peer assessment
Reflective journal	Recorded audio submission	Practical assignment
		Simulation

Figure 5.4 List of possible assessment methods

Selection of the right kind of assessment is of great importance when you consider the process of centre-based assessment design. It must fulfil the criteria that we have looked at earlier.

In addition to the criteria for assessment, the very essence of vocational learning is in the development of a range of skills that will prove useful in the workplace, in this case the travel and tourism workplace. So the format must have wider-ranging potential and be vocationally relevant, stimulating and challenging

Awarding bodies generally suggest a range of assessment tools, but almost always point those designing assessments to be innovative, creative and to design assessment to fit their own local needs.

Reflection 5.9

Having reflected on the list of possible assessment 'tools' in Figure 5.4 and perhaps added some of your own, now turn to the list of programme outcomes in Figure 5.5 and try to decide what you think would be the most appropriate assessment tool for each one.

Remember to apply the principles of validity, reliability and authenticity to your choice.

- Complete travel services bookings (level 2)
- Receive, prepare and issue travel documentation (level 2)
- Know the components of travel and tourism and how they interrelate (level 3)
- Understand how recent developments have shaped the present day travel and tourism industry (level 3)
- Understand how hospitality providers meet customer expectations (level 3)
- Understand the appeal of visitor attractions to different types of visitor (level 3)
- Be able to demonstrate customer service skills in travel and tourism situations (level 3)
- Be able to organize a promotional campaign for a travel and tourism organization (level 3)
- Know Health and Safety legislation affecting employees, customers, property, health and hygiene (level 2)
- Learn and give examples of different types of tourist destinations in the UK (level 2)
- Give a definition of ecotourism (level 2)
- Identify different sales situations in leisure and tourism (level 2)
- Understand how unforeseen and uncontrollable events such as the global credit crunch may influence or bring about change in the leisure and tourism industry (level 2)

Figure 5.5 List of possible programme outcomes

Assessment for learning

Although, for the most part we have tried to address the issues of assessment *of* learning, which tends to be *summative,* we did briefly touch on formative assessment or assessment *for* learning both in our introduction to this chapter and in Chapter 4. That this is an essential element of the learning process is, generally, undisputed. Black and Wiliam in their small but much quoted booklet, *Inside the Black Box,* suggest that this means, 'An assessment activity [that] can help learning if it provides information to be used as feedback, by teachers and their pupils, to modify the teaching and learning activities in which they are engaged' (1998: 5).

Giving feedback

Earlier, we also observed how feedback is, of course, essential to the process of learning, whether it is internalized by the learner analysing his or her own performance, or if it comes from an external person such as a peer or a teacher. By assessing the actual outcomes of our efforts and matching them to the intended outcomes, we can, if necessary, modify our behaviour or work to meet with success. So it is most important that we include space for feedback at several intervals in our assessment plan and, again, this should be included in our scheme of work.

There is little that can be more demotivating to a learner than negative feedback, that is, feedback that only focuses on the faults, for we can learn as much from our successes as from our faults, and possibly more. So, feedback should be supportive and adapted to the specific learner's needs, guiding them to recognize what they have achieved and encouraging them to extend themselves more. It could also include an opportunity for the learner to have an input, through questioning, so they develop a critical stance to their own work and, incidentally, hone their skills of autonomous learning.

Reflection 5.10

In Chapter 3, we asked you to mark a piece of work from a student who had written quite competently about tourist destinations, but who needed help with their literacy skills (Figure 3.1).

With the benefit of what you have now read, write some feedback which is at once encouraging yet also developmental.

This means that it should read a little more positively than, 'Good content: poor use of language'!

Verification and moderation: quality management

Finally, we should ask the question, 'How do I know that my assessment plan or assignment is acceptable to the awarding body, the institution and, of course, the learners?'

The learners will let you know soon enough if they cannot understand the assignment, or if they think that it does not reflect the intended learning outcomes, but what of the other stakeholders? If this is your first attempt at designing assessment, there should be help at hand through a process of internal and external verification and moderation. Although the two may sometimes be confused and the distinction between them blurred, essentially verification implies a bureaucratic authentication or rubber stamping, whereas moderation suggests a less formal process of comparison and standardization of grading: a discussion between assessors and an experienced, appointed moderator.

Although different centres may have different quality management systems, there will generally be a fully qualified internal verifier whose role it is to critically examine all assessments before they are presented to learners. They will, of course, check that it fulfils all the criteria for the proposed unit of assessment and that it conforms to the principles of assessment that we have discussed at some length. This verifier should be prepared to advise you even before you embark on the process of design.

When the assessment has been graded and moderated by the programme team through a process of cross-grading and discussion, the internal verifier will sample a cross-section of assessments and agree upon appropriate standards.

The whole process is monitored carefully by the awarding bodies through a system of external moderators who do the same job as the internal verifier, checking assessment briefs and standardizing grading but, of course, with reference to a wide range of other centres, thus ensuring reliability in the assessment practices of each centre. It is their role to judge the efficacy of the internal verification systems and in this respect their role is a critical one; if there are major discrepancies in the verification and moderation systems, they have the power to block a centre's authority to grant certification to learners completing their programmes.

Summary

A central theme to this chapter has been to try to view assessment as an essential element in the process of learning. It is our way of finding out, in the first instance, what our learners bring to the learning environment (diagnostic assessment), and then what they learn either as they progress through the programme of learning (formative assessment) or at the end (summative assessment). Essentially it is about judging 'the quality of student achievement' (Armitage and Renwick 2008: 5).

The role of feedback is seen as central to this learning process, whether it is based on our own self-assessment or that of another person, a peer or a teacher. How else can we know about the quality of our learning? So we have considered how this feedback can best be supportive of learning and have decided that it must first focus on the positive elements of the outcomes of the assessment before addressing any areas for improvement.

However, it is just as important that the assessment activities by which we make these judgements are equal to the task of measuring what it is that we hope the students have learnt. We have, therefore, looked at the principles that underpin assessment design and at the methods and tools currently at our disposal.

Assessment design should be seen to be relevant to the learners' needs and to the content and context of the programme. It should, in other words, be a valid assessment reflecting the realities of their programmes in the wider world of travel and tourism, whether that be in an occupational role, such as for an NVQ, or in higher education as an academic field of study. It should be a means by which our learners can demonstrate the quality of their learning, not an instrument designed to find out their deficiencies.

Finally, we have tried to contextualize assessment within the various programmes on which our learners will have enrolled and have noted the differences in the ways that they are assessed. On the one hand, NVQs will assess practical skills, although, as we have seen, even they have an element of knowledge and understanding: it is not enough to be able to 'Make a booking for travel services', agents need to know 'The main responsibilities under current industry codes of practice and legislation' (The City and Guilds of London 2005: 35 and 36). On the other hand, A level or Foundation Degree travel and tourism will demand in-depth study of a variety of academic aspects of travel and tourism such as the environmental and social impacts of tourism, and this might best be tested through examinations. Then again, we have programmes, such as National Diplomas, assessed by continuous coursework requiring our students to develop skills as autonomous learners.

We hope that this will have helped you to develop not only a range of strategies for assessment but also a rationale for your choice. Perhaps, too, it will have motivated you to find ways of creating models that will make the process of assessment a more enjoyable, stimulating and challenging experience for your learners.

6

Maximizing the use of resources in travel and tourism

In this chapter we will be looking at:

- how resources can support learning and teaching in the travel and tourism curriculum
- identifying and preparing resources appropriate to the needs of learners
- the teacher as resource
- developing resources to support classroom teaching
- resources that enhance autonomous learning, such as textbooks and Internet access
- resourcing learning and teaching in the varied learning environments of the travel and tourism sector
- making links and partnerships with travel and tourism organizations and practitioners to enhance the learning experience including educational visits
- making the most of the work placement as a resource.

Using resources to support learning and teaching in the travel and tourism curriculum

Well-prepared and appropriate resources are an important aid to support, motivate and reinforce learning in any subject, and this is certainly true of the travel and tourism curriculum. We have seen in Chapter 1 how our learners are generally active participants and this means that, in a classroom environment, it is particularly important that they are engaged in active learning which, in turn, will most likely involve the use of stimulating resources. On the other hand, many of our teaching and learning activities will be of a practical nature which will involve management of specialist environments to maximize their potential as learning resources.

For our purposes, we have found it convenient to consider resources for travel and tourism under these two categories: the classroom in which we generally address theoretical topics and the wider environments where we engage in experiential learning, the practical application of theory and applied learning. The latter would include environments such as the tourist attractions, town and city landscapes, flight decks and fuselages, and travel centres. However, this is not to say that these should be considered as separate, unrelated environments: the one complements the other. Practical activities should be informed by theory, and practical activity is the way in which we test the validity of the theory. So we need to ensure that resources for practical activities are adequate to support the application of theory.

In the classroom, we consider first how resources can support the teacher in preparing meaningful learning experiences, and then how we deploy these resources to develop our students as autonomous learners. We see how modern electronic technology has changed our classrooms, but will also acknowledge the use of non-electronic resources, such as textbooks, journals, hard-copy handouts and pen boards.

The wider travel and tourism environments are too vast to consider each separately within this publication, so our focus is more generally on how to make the most of them in terms of experiential learning, which we discussed in Chapter 4.

Finally, as we also briefly mentioned in Chapter 4, nowhere provides a more realistic environment better than the workplace, so we address the planning of educational visits and work placements as an essential resource for the teacher of travel and tourism. We might add here the value of inviting speakers to share their current experiences in the industry with your classes.

As we have seen in Chapter 2, the syllabus, the scheme of work and the lesson plan are your starting point for planning. Here we explore resources that assist in taking the learning objectives off the page to become a learning experience.

Resources that enhance learning and teaching in the classroom

Creating a stimulating learning environment

In Chapter 4 we saw how one teacher turned an unpromising learning environment into one which set the scene for her lesson on Greece, using posters and music to create a learning environment to stimulate interest in the topic in her learners. Opportunities abound in travel and tourism to turn our classrooms into exciting centres of learning for our students. Travel agencies and tourist information centres will willingly pass on posters and brochures that they no longer have a use for, and we can hide those plain magnolia-painted walls with colourful images, maps and even photographs of our learners studying in various destinations. Although this does provide an opportunity to familiarize your learners with destinations they have never been to, the theme does not always have to be based on an exotic one: your local area can provide equally interesting material. Indeed, the learners themselves should be tasked with creating the display as a part of their own development as autonomous learners. This does not have to be an expensive exercise. A collection of tourist attraction leaflets may provide a number of different learning activities, such as identifying demographic groups, learning geography, identifying regional products, mapping travel routes, itinerary planning, recognizing the different organizational sectors or reviewing disabled facilities, to name just a few. If you have a dedicated room, then it may even be possible to set up a part of it as a small travel agency with brochures and reference books, guides and timetables, and even a personal computer for researching and booking travel arrangements.

The teacher as a resource

There is probably no more important resource in any of the learning environments discussed so far than you, the teacher. The effectiveness of the programme effectively revolves around your own wealth of expertise and knowledge. As a teacher of travel and tourism, you are expected to maintain an in-depth knowledge of the subject, just as in any other. There is no better way to keep up to date with current developments than to take out a regular subscription to the *Travel Trade Gazette* which should be regarded as essential reading for all teachers of travel and tourism.

> **Reflection 6.1**
>
> Thinking about the breadth of your own experiences in travel and tourism as a client, employee or student, take a few moments to consider what you can offer to your students to enhance their knowledge and understanding of the industry.

However, even knowing that we are the experts in our subject, there are few other subjects that feature so largely in the public domain as travel and tourism, as we saw in Chapter 1. Nearly everyone enrolled on your programmes, of whatever age, will have a view informed at least by the media and, possibly, in-depth experience of travelling the world. The answer to this challenge is to ensure that when you enter a classroom you are fully prepared. Your subject knowledge must be of sufficient depth to ensure that you can use the teaching skills you are developing to make each lesson a valuable learning experience. This chapter will assist in ensuring that your knowledge is up to date and accurate. Remember that when you say something as a teacher, there is an expectation (quite rightly) that you know what you are talking about.

You may have a degree in the subject and/or some experience from working in the industry. This helps you understand topic areas of the travel and tourism subject syllabus, but do not fall into the trap of planning all your lessons only around the areas you know; your role is to bring the whole syllabus (and industry if appropriate) to the learning experience. Your own learning must continue for you to do this. Sources of information are vast, including textbooks, television, the Internet, DVDs, industry organizations, work shadowing and visiting speakers, so be prepared to engage with them all in the process of your own professional development. If you work in the lifelong learning sector, you will know that this is now a part of your contract, a requirement of your membership of the Institute for Learning. In schools, too, you will be expected to undertake continuing professional development.

Reflection 6.2

Thinking about some of the issues discussed in Chapter 1, what do you think are the most recent developments in the travel and tourism industry?

How confident are you that your subject knowledge is up to date?

How could you update your knowledge and understanding of current policies and practices in the industry?

The learners

While the teacher and visiting speakers might have a wider experience of the travel and tourism industry, we should also value the experiences that our learners bring to the programme. As we have seen, some may have some experience of travel and tourism through experience of family holidays, days out or school trips and most will have been influenced by the media. The travel and tourism industry is well represented in the media through advertising, travel programmes, reality shows and even comedy shows such as *Benidorm*. Some learners will indeed have travelled through family ties; you may find that some have travelled more extensively than yourself. The expert teacher will be able to draw on these experiences to enhance the learning of the whole group.

Reflection 6.3

Jason's parents have been working around the world and have lived in many European cities. He has attended schools in these cities.

At college, he was studying for a BTEC National in Travel and Tourism.

What aspects of his life might a teacher be able to draw upon to enhance the learning experience of the whole group?

How could the teacher integrate this into the learning programme?

Reflection 6.4

Claire has a daytime job as a financial consultant and is a volunteer at her local National Trust property. She has been studying a Foundation Degree in Leisure and Tourism for some years now and is hoping to qualify and work as a manager at a National Trust property.

What special knowledge and understanding might she be able to contribute to the class?

How might you try to integrate this into your lessons?

Resources that support teaching and learning

We have frequently made reference to the fact that, if our teaching is to be meaningful for our learners, then we should be creating interactive learning environments that stimulate and engage them, and the way that we use resources to support our lessons has an important role to play in this process. Here we shall first consider resources based on electronic technology and then non-electronic resources.

Resources based on electronic technology

The pace of technological change has seen a rapid growth in the development of electronic resources that can give us easy and instant access to information and support tools that can make our teaching more stimulating for our learners, particularly the younger adults for many of whom such technology is an accepted part of their everyday life. As teachers we should not be fearful of these developments but should embrace them, and use our learners' knowledge and understanding of them to our advantage. On the other hand, we should also be aware that not all learners have such ready access to this technology when away from the institution and that they could be at a disadvantage were we to assume that they can work independently at home. Also, as we saw in Chapter 3, some may be fearful of modern technology and might need considerable support to develop even basic skills, particularly more mature adults.

However, it is fast becoming the norm to use technological resources such as PowerPoint in the classroom to support the teacher's presentation, so we will now consider how make the best use of some of these, with the proviso that, by the time of publication, the likelihood is that we shall already be out of date.

Using PowerPoint presentations

The importance and strength of a PowerPoint presentation (or, the Apple Mac version, Keynote) is that it will help to reinforce learning by providing a visual stimulus. Whether we accept the principle of learning styles, that we are fulfilling the needs of the visual learner, or are, like Coffield et al. (2004), more sceptical (see Chapter 4), the visual impact of PowerPoint does underpin and provide a focus to our delivery. It will identify key words and ideas that the learner can note down and, used creatively with illustrations, can be a potent aid to learning. Figure 6.1, overleaf is an example of a PowerPoint slide.

Reflection 6.5

What are the key features of the slide shown in Figure 6.1?

What are its main flaws (if there are any)?

Would you have designed this differently?

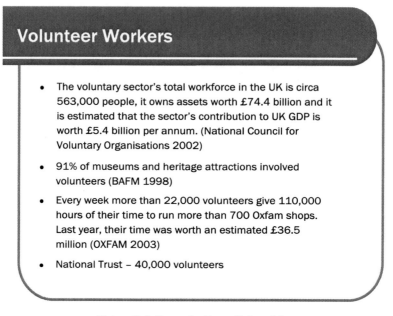

Figure 6.1 Exemplar PowerPoint slide

Furthermore, the potential of PowerPoint can be considerably enhanced by the introduction of hyperlinks. These links will enable you and the learner to access websites and video clips for supplementary information at the click of a mouse! It is not within the scope of this publication to instruct the reader in these processes, but programs such as PowerPoint have inbuilt instructions that are easy to follow: you can insert a hyperlink to Internet websites. When you show the presentation to a class, you can click on the link and enhance your lesson with references to video clips.

Problems with PowerPoint

Reflection 6.6

You may remember the most ineffective PowerPoint presentation that you've suffered – even if you can't remember what it was about, often they are the most memorable.

Why was it a poor example of this medium?

What features needed to be improved?

PowerPoint can be a very potent tool, but it is not without its pitfalls. The 'death by PowerPoint' syndrome is well known in education and training circles. Presentations of 40 or 50 slides are not unknown, and this can be counterproductive. Instead of stimulating the learner, this is more likely to send them to sleep! It would suggest that the presenter is relying on the slides for the content of the session and possibly merely reading from them rather than using them as a stimulus. This is hardly inter-active teaching and learning: the PowerPoint presentation should be used to support learning not replace it.

The slide in our example gives important, yet minimal information which is helpfully bullet-pointed, leaving the teacher and the learner to fill in the gaps through question and answer and discussion. In an overcrowded slide, the important points can easily be lost. Furthermore, your slides will be much more memorable and interesting if they are illustrated by importing pictures from clip-art or perhaps photographs.

Important guidelines then would be:

- Do not use too many slides.
- Do not overcrowd any slide with information.
- Make the slides memorable where possible by using illustrations.
- Insert hyperlinks to make a wider range of information accessible. Some that are useful to the teacher of travel and tourism may be found at the end of this chapter.

Making your presentations accessible to your learners
There is a tendency for audiences at a presentation, whether in your class or at a conference, to want to write down everything they see on the slides. However, this is unnecessary and distracting for them, and can be pre-empted by copying the presentation onto an internal website such as Blackboard or Moodle and making this available to your learners, perhaps with the warning that downloading the presentation is no substitute for attending your lessons!

Of course, it is also possible to print off hard copies with space for making notes (Figure 6.2). This has the advantage that, should the technology fail or not be available, you will still be able to use the presentation albeit in a much more limited fashion. The problem here is to know when to give out the hard-copy handouts. You want the learners to have them available to make notes that complement the presentation, yet if you give them out too early, they will perhaps read ahead of your input and not focus on the discussion in hand. One way of dealing with this is to give out the pages of the handout in stages rather than all at once at the beginning.

Interactive whiteboards (IWBs)
An interactive whiteboard is essentially a multi-layered surface which will accept the display of a projector or camera. It is activated either by touch of hand or a stylus. It will allow you and learners the ability to draw, write and create unique documents, and save them as part of a recognizable text document for whatever reason.

Consider the advantage to the travel and tourism learner who can import images from the Internet of destinations or examples of good customer service video clips. Because everything created can be saved, it means that whole lessons can be captured and retrieved at any point, potentially particularly useful for absentees or for revision.

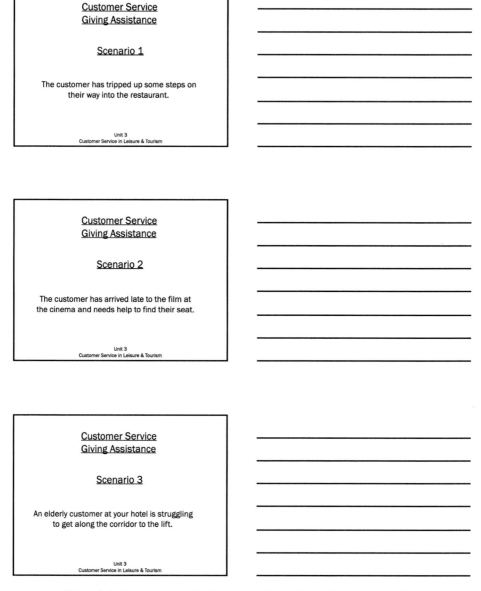

Figure 6.2 Exemplar handout for supporting a PowerPoint presentation

Interactive whiteboards can deliver contemporary, exciting interactivities across an expanding range of subject areas such as for marketing five principles.

The use of these boards is now widespread and expanding, and it is claimed that their use enables learners to understand new concepts and for the tutor to plan and to engage all learners.

Video, DVD and CDs

The filming and projection of moving images is an invaluable resource in bringing travel and tourism to life in the classroom and there are a number of applications of which we can take advantage. The filming of role play of customer service, air cabin service or tour operators' 'welcome' meetings, will allow both learner and teacher to review the work.

Reflection 6.7

Before we discuss this further, you could spend a few moments coming up with a few ideas of your own. Perhaps you already are an expert user of moving images: please try to recall all the different ways that you have used them to enhance learning or to supplement your own attempts at describing some difficult concept.

Video clips of tourism destinations might be used to illustrate particular aspects of a topic, such as the impact of tourism on a destination. Also, there are a number of commercially produced resources illustrating different types of holiday, such as cruising, all of which can help you in your explanations of what otherwise can seem to be rather mysterious to the learner and can be difficult to describe, particularly if your class is not well travelled or if holidays are only sand and sea based rather than exploring unique destinations. Your local travel agency is a good place to locate such resources.

However, as always, there is a note of caution: the video is not a substitute for your teaching. It should be used to enhance learning and should be accompanied by preparation and debrief as always in order to contextualize the topic. While watching yet another episode of *Fawlty Towers* may be engaging, funny and entertaining for your class, it has no real significance unless discussed in the context of customer service or even of management skills.

Video cameras and mobile phones

Cameras of a very reasonable quality are relatively cheap now and are easy to use. Many of your learners will be quite expert in their use and you may find that their mobile phones have this facility. Since younger adults, at least, appear to be addicted to the 'mobile', why not put them to constructive use?

Creating your own videos can be a most useful tool, especially to enhance your travel and tourism programmes: making a video of your local area can give an insight into tour guiding. Perhaps as we have already seen the most important use is to record performance, perhaps a role play or group presentation. This can then be played back for analysis or even for assessment. Indeed, creating a video might even *be* the assessment method.

Reflection 6.8

How many ways could you use video to assess performance in a travel and tourism programme?

How could a learner-produced video be used as an alternative means of assessment for an assignment?

Other non-electronic resources

Unfortunately, the technology is not necessarily always as reliable or available as we might like it to be, so it is always important to have an alternative resource at hand and to retain the skills to use it.

White (pen) boards

Where interactive boards are not available, generally there will be a whiteboard on which you can write with the appropriate marker pens. Again, this is still an important resource to promote interactive learning. It allows you to write up learner responses to questions, thus showing that you value their contribution. It enables you respond in the moment to the development of the lesson, perhaps developing a model to structure information, as already suggested, in the form of a flow chart. It allows you to write up key words that your learners will need to know for that lesson and to note lesson objectives that they can check during the session.

Flip charts

Board work can often be complemented or even substituted by the use of a flip chart. It can be useful to record information (such as key words or lesson objectives) that you want to retain throughout the session and that might otherwise be rubbed off the board.

However, the flip chart is a flexible resource that has another important role in the interactive lesson. It can be used so that the learners can, generally in group work, create posters to display their responses to discussions as a focus to presentations. These can then be displayed on the classroom walls as a reminder of the outcomes of their work.

Handouts

We have already referred to handouts as a way of distributing our PowerPoint presentations to learners. However, they clearly have a wider use. They can provide supplementary information gleaned from a variety of sources such as articles photocopied from journals, maps, photographs of destinations and summaries of important aspects of a lesson. As with the PowerPoint presentation, overload should be avoided: learners are far more likely to read something that is relatively uncluttered and if there is not too much paper involved.

Handouts will be of much greater value if they are used as a stimulus to learning and are accompanied by questions perhaps to ensure that the learners do actually refer to them.

A development of the handout is the 'gapped handout' in which key words are left out for the learner to complete. This can be particularly useful to make notes from a presentation where the teacher has provided a certain amount of information but has left out phrases or words, the answer to which will be found in during the presentation.

Resources that enhance autonomous learning

So far we have considered resources that enable the teacher to develop an interactive environment with their learners. However, for the learner to take greater responsibility for their own learning, they need to be able to access sources of information that will develop their knowledge and understanding, and have the means to produce a record of their findings. Clearly, electronic sources will feature highly in this, but so will paper sources such as books, journals and magazines.

Textbooks

Publications that will support the development of the learner range from workbooks for GCSE learners to engage in question and answer exercises, such as *Classroom Activities for AQA GCSE Leisure and Tourism* (Carden 2009) and the *Student Book for AQA, OCR, WJEC and CCEA* (Canwell and Sutherland 2003), to general textbooks that are written to give an overview of the industry such as Stephen Page's (2007) *Tourism Management*, or Chris Cooper et al.'s (2008) *Tourism: Principles and Practice*, with exercises and activities (see Figure 6.3, overleaf) to encourage learners to reflect and research.

While these publications are invaluable sources of information and can help the teacher with their planning, there is a danger that the learner will become too reliant on them. The danger is that they will look no further and that this will result in the 'surface learning' that we discussed in Chapter 4. They will consider that the 'answers' that they need to pass the assignment are all in the book and will reproduce the information just as set out therein. The teacher is then left with the daunting task of marking large numbers of assignments that all appear to be the same and with no real originality. Clearly, the way in which assignments are written, as discussed in Chapter 5, must ensure that the learner is encouraged to reflect on experience and research more widely.

One valuable aid which no travel teacher can afford to be without, when teaching GSCE, A level and ABTAC, is the *Travel Trade Atlas* published annually by Columbus Press. This book provides extensive up to-date information, transport routes, geography statistics plus many other important facts about travel. This publisher has other texts, wall maps and teaching materials that further support teaching and which are well worth reviewing.

Internet access

There are two important ways in which you can use Internet resources as a teacher. First, you can use them to support your own work in preparing your programmes and lessons and, second, their use can be embedded into your programmes to enhance learning and to enable your learners to research sources for information.

Activity 3: Comparing organisations

Produce a poster or presentation slide that compares the promotional activities and sales activities of your two orgranisations (used in Activities 1 and 2).

Your may present this as a table or come up with a more creative way!

To help you complete this task, think about the following points:

- The similarities in the organisations' sales activities – e.g. do they both sell their products via the internet, face-to-face, etc.
- The differences in the organisations' sales activities – e.g. one organisation may have a call centre to take bookings whereas the other may require customers to go into the facility to purchase the service, etc.
- The promotional techniques that they both use;
- The differences in the techniques that they choose to use, e.g. one organisation may use advertising a great deal as they are a multinational chain, whereas the other organisation may rely more on public relations (PR) as they have a very limited budget;
- The promotional materials that both organisations use;
- How the promotional materials differ between the two organisations, e.g. for advertising, one organisation may use high-powered TV advertisements as they are a multinational company, whereas the other organisation may rely more on local newspaper adverts as their target market is their local community.

Activity 4: Target markets

A 'target market' is made up of all the customers that an organisation is trying to attract to use or buy its products and services. The market can be split into different sections/parts that are called 'market segments'. The total market can be segmented using a range of different factors.

a.   Complete the following diagram by adding the correct letters to make a range of factors that can be used to segment a market for a leisure and tourism product:

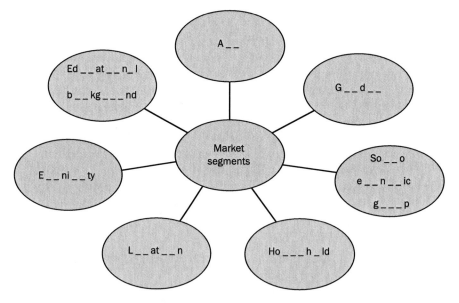

Figure 6.3 Exemplar workbook activities (Carden 2009. Reproduced from *Classroom Activities for AQA GCSE Leisure & Tourism* (Catherine Carden: ISBN 9780956268020) with the permission of Travel & Tourism Publishing Ltd.)

Supporting teaching through the Internet

In the first instance, there are a number of websites designed by teachers for teachers and dedicated to sharing information about educational resources, within which you will be able to access subject-specific information. These are generally called 'gateway' sites since they provide you with routes to other useful resources. Specially recommended by Geoff Petty (2009: 405) are the following:

> http://excellence.qia.org.uk/
> www.intute.ac.uk/
> www.bbc.co.uk/learning/
> www.curriculumonline.gov.uk/

We would add:

> http://www.bized.co.uk/
> http://teachers.net/
> http://www.lsnlearning.org.uk/
> http://www.wrl-ne.com/teaching-and-learning-resources/lesuire-tourism
> http://www.wordle.net/ (is good for starters/plenaries)
> http://delicious.com/ (bookmarking site to issue reading to students and so on)
> http://www.teachers-direct.co.uk/resources/quiz%2Dbusters/

Subject-specific sites

Springboard UK /Career Scope: which has a resource gateway specifically for hospitality, leisure, travel and tourism. Springboard also provides access to industry related summer schools well as selling teaching resources (http://education.springboarduk.net/).

UKSP: which, has many resources free to both teacher and learner (http://www.uksp.co.uk).

Tourism Concern: also has many in-depth case studies and other resources regarding the impacts of tourism (http://www.tourismconcern.org.uk).
Finally, but not exhaustively, the site provided by the Higher Education Academy, Hospitality, Leisure, Sport and Tourism Network which aims to encourage and broker the sharing of good learning and teaching practice (http://www.heacademy.ac.uk/hlst/ourwork/heinfe/teachingexchange).

Supporting learning through the Internet

The second way that we can use the Internet is to embed its use into our schemes of work and lesson plans (see Chapters 2, 3 and 4), thus encouraging our learners to use it constructively to develop their knowledge and understanding while also developing their key and functional skills.

There are also, of course, problems with managing the 'virtual learning environment'. Our younger students in particular will be familiar with ICT and many use it for playing games and communication. Constant vigilance is required to ensure that they remain 'on task' and that they are not distracted by attractive alternatives.

The amount of information available through the Internet is vast and is an invaluable tool to enhance your students' learning. The problem is being able to refine the research. Of course, your learners can use a search engine but typing in 'National Parks' on Google, for example, will give you 160 million entries. Of course, refining this to the UK will reduce the entries considerably but there are still far too many to process easily, so it is useful to build up a database of websites of your own or access a 'gateway' site that has already done the job for you: there is one such useful site provided by Coventry University providing many links to sites useful to you on www.stile.coventry.ac.uk/cbs/stafff/beech/tourism.

There are many organizations that provide educational materials to support the teaching of travel and tourism. Some of the more general sites are identified in the Appendix, however, many individual sites such as tourist attractions have educational support materials, such as, the Visit Liverpool website education section 'Merseywise' at http://www.visitliverpool.com/merseywise/home. This site has case studies based on local tourism related to both GSCE, and A Level and higher education subject teaching.

Virtual learning environments (VLEs)

As technology reshapes forever the way in which education is delivered, assessed and even managed, the evolution of the virtual learning environment is perhaps the most significant innovation in recent times.

For more than ten years educationalists have explored the notion of a web-based platform that could allow the storage for easy access of a range of teaching and learning materials, perhaps the most important role of the VLE thus far. Effectively it is a software package that allows the assessor, by remote access, the ability to access tools such as assessment graders, test-setting software, electronic assessment or return of student work via the VLE, or perhaps less formally a basis of inexpensive electronic communication via forums. In addition to this the VLE also allows the learner the ability to access lecture notes, assessment activities and peer communication and present the submission of coursework by remote and secure access.

From an organizational point of view it is fast becoming a tool for learner survey with a data bank of a variety of useful institutional data about remote access and interactivity.

Many centres are now subscribed to VLEs such as Fronter and Moodle, which boast a range of possibilities such as initial diagnostic assessment, or perhaps more excitingly the unprecedented opportunity for the sharing of resources across sector education areas.

People as resources

Visiting speakers

Visiting speakers who are currently working in the travel and tourism environment will help to contextualize your learners' studies. There are many organizations whose staff, such as the local tourist attraction managers, destination development managers or travel agency staff, are happy either to provide speakers or to offer visits. As we observed in Chapter 4, the trick here is that your preparation provides an experience to meet learning outcomes. The preparation should begin by ensuring that the timing of a talk from an 'industry expert' is complementary to your scheme of work. It is also necessary to ensure that the speaker is aware of your planned learning outcomes and how their contribution fits with these outcomes. A speaker for a speaker's sake will very quickly lose you credibility with your learning group, particularly with older groups of learners.

As a safety check you should ensure the speaker is comfortable talking to large groups and knows to whom they will be speaking, their audience. People not familiar with teaching may need guidance. For example, if it is a young group, the speaker may need to adjust their use of language to an appropriate level, so that it is neither too complicated nor too simple. If jargon is going to be used, it should be explained: people who work with jargon tend to forget the rest of the world does not understand it. It is helpful to display key words on a board or chart. You should perhaps advise the speaker to consider carefully if what they are going to say will be acceptable or perhaps be found funny or embarrassing by a group of teenagers. The presentation needs to be in a logical order that will not confuse the learners; the speaker may require some of your expert help in preparing the talk to ensure clarity of message.

Most importantly, you will need to confirm that the speaker provides the outcomes the learners require from the talk; an interesting talk does not always translate into a report on customer service, which the group have to produce for the assessment. Time spent preparing the speaker will overcome issues later.

Preparation of the learners will further maximize the learning outcomes from the occasion. If the talk is carefully planned into your scheme of work, the relevance and context will be apparent to the learners. However, can you enhance the learning by preparing resources, such as a gapped handout with headings under which topics spoken about can be captured, which may be completed immediately after the presentation. Be wary of expecting the learners to remember what the speaker said in the lesson a week previously.

Preparation using the syllabus or assessment criteria or with the learners' contributions to understanding the learning process

Preparing pupils through an exercise where they generate their own questions to which they require answers from the syllabus or assessment criteria may help their development as autonomous learners by:

- focusing on the outcome needed for learning or assessment
- developing the learners' own planning and learning skills.

Having secured your speaker it is important to make the experience enjoyable for them too, so they will support you in future. Your learners need to show respect for the speaker who has given up their time to address them and, importantly, interact with them in an intelligent manner. Visitors coming in from outside the educational environment wish to feel valued: silence by a group may be seen as a lack of valuing the experience. Thus it is important during the planning process to ensure that the learners prepare their questions to maximize the benefits gained from the occasion.

Reflection 6.9

You have booked the manager of the local council tourist information centre to give a presentation on customer service to your Advanced Diploma group of mainly 16- to 17-year-olds.

What measures would you take to prepare the speaker:

(a)   to cover the learning outcomes?
(b)   to help them relate to the group?

Finally, you need to ensure that all technology is working before commencement of the talk: it can be very embarrassing for a speaker whose presentation is focused on PowerPoint slides to find that the projector is not working.

Remember you must ask permission from the appropriate authorities to bring a visitor into a school or college; that the person may not be Criminal Record Bureau checked and so should not, in that case, be left alone with your class.

External organizations

Again, in Chapter 4 we considered the importance of practical experience in the occupational environment. In this respect, making links with employers, although time consuming, is a valuable exercise and offers great rewards.

Establishing good relationships with managers of local travel agencies, tourist attractions or local authority museums can open all kinds of opportunities. We have seen how they may be willing to give presentations to your learners but, better still, they may be prepared to show you all round their facility and give a talk on site.

Furthermore, you may be able to make an arrangement for your groups to use the facilities either informally or as a part of the programme and, of course, they may provide another outlet for work-based learning.

Teaching outside the classroom

As a teacher of travel and tourism you will have to consider taking pupils/students out of the classroom. It could be an expectation of your employment; it certainly will enhance your teaching and your learner's experience. This could range from a visit to the local town centre to an overseas residential field trip. In all cases there are a number of issues you have to consider from a teaching and learning perspective and a personal perspective.

The Royal Society for the Prevention of Accidents (ROSPA) advises:

Teachers are obliged to take all reasonable measures to ensure that every child under their control and supervision is safe and protected from any unacceptable risks. The teacher must be CAREFUL not CARELESS. Being careless is, in legal terms, being negligent; and being negligent means that you might be liable. (ROSPA 2001)

On the other hand, however, the DfES advised that, 'The school curriculum should . . . enable pupils to respond positively to opportunities, challenges and responsibilities, to manage risk and to cope with change and adversity' (DfES and QCA 1999: 3).

The dilemma for the teacher of travel and tourism, then, is how to maintain the balance for our learners by ensuring that, while providing every opportunity for them to experience the external environment in the widest possible contexts, they also take every precaution to minimize the risks.

Clearly some environments involve more risks than others. At the extreme end of a continuum from low risk to high, we should be aware of the inherent risks in travel and tourism involving adventurous outdoor activities such as skiing or canoeing. The ROSPA gives the following examples of potential dangers and the outcomes:

- Four children lost their lives when they were swept out to sea off the rocks at Land's End; four boys died when they slid over a precipice in Austria;
- Four sixth formers died in a canoeing accident at Lyme Bay in Dorset;
- Twelve children and a teacher died when their minibus crashed into the back of a maintenance vehicle on the hard shoulder of the M40.

As a result of any tragic incident involving school children, questions are asked, procedures are tightened, and new legislation may come into force. A case in point is the *Activity Centres (Young Person's Safety) Act 1995* and the *Adventure Activities Licensing Regulations* 1996 which resulted from the Lyme Bay incident.

The ROSPA website (www.rospa.com/safetyeducation/schooltrips/part2.htm, accessed 7 Feb. 2010), provides excellent advice for making such field trips safer.

Nobody would suggest that these are common accidents but, by definition, they are unexpected and probably arising from apparently innocuous situations. The teacher needs to be constantly aware of the dangers.

Planning the educational field visit

Before planning a visit, for groups of all ages whether young or more mature adults, there must be effective planning for this teaching strategy just as there is in classroom-based methods.

First, we need to make sure that the visit is meaningful and will enhance learning for our groups. It is worth repeating that it should provide an opportunity to contextualize learning and to experience the reality of the travel and tourism environment. It should, therefore, be driven by the learning outcomes identified in our schemes of work and provide opportunities for our learners to achieve them. Again, they should be carefully prepared, in much the same way as we recommended for the visiting speakers so that their purpose is clear.

Then, of course, there is the organization of the visit for which most organizations will have a clear set of guidelines and protocols. Sometimes this can take longer than we might wish since the agreement of a number of stakeholders has first to be established, so the importance of forward planning through the scheme of work is, again, essential.

Figure 6.4 sets out a schedule of planning that you might find a useful guide to helping to make the visit an enjoyable, safe and meaningful learning experience.

Planning the Educational Visit

1. **Appraise the benefits:**
   Is your trip really necessary? Senior managers, parents and learners need to know what the intended learning outcomes are.

2. **Check the institutional protocols:**
   What permissions are necessary? What forms are there to complete? How much notice is required? What are the conditions of the insurance cover?

3. **Identify any potential risks:**
   See previous discussion on risks but this can also include the prevailing weather conditions. It may be very hot or very cold at the destination: will the group be sufficiently prepared for this?

4. **Identify participants' needs:**
   Are there any health, dietary or fitness issues? Field trips can involve a lot of walking – are all members of the group up to it? Will there be any mobility issues (e.g. wheelchair access)? Take home contact numbers.

5. **Ratio of staff to students:**
   Check the protocols: 1:15 for trips at home 1:10 abroad. Take account of the gender mix, any special needs and the level of risk involved.

6. **Transport and accommodation:**
   Plan the itinerary in detail and inform participants. Take special care if public transport is used: the London Underground can be daunting! If possible, check accommodation beforehand for health and safety and also proximity to other guests: a group of excited young adults can be irritating!

7. **Excursions:**
   Again, these should be well planned with clear objectives and the cost included in the overall package.

While on the trip

1. **Behaviour:**
   Expectations should be laid down beforehand and participants should sign an agreement and possible sanctions made clear. Be aware that alcohol can be a problem, and have clear policies about this.

2. **Keeping track of the group:**
   All members of the group must have an itinerary and contact numbers should they get lost (for once, mobile phones are invaluable!). Be aware and check numbers frequently.

3. **Unplanned events including possible injuries:**
   Make sure that you have contingency plans including emergency cash or credit, someone who is First Aid trained and a Senior management home contact.

Figure 6.4 Protocols for planning the educational visit

Reflection 6.10

Using the schedule of planning for an educational visit (Figure 6.4), draft out a plan for one (or both) of the visits suggested below, maximizing the benefits and minimizing the risks:

(a) Plan to take a group of learners with which you are familiar to a major tourist attraction of your own choice for a day visit. The group might be 14-year-olds studying for GCSE or a diploma, 17- to 19-year-olds on a National Diploma programme or mature adults on a management programme, or any other group of your choosing. The visit might be to Alton Towers, or a local National Trust property, or a national park; again the choice is yours.

(b) Plan to take a group (again, of any age) on a residential visit to a European city. They are largely inexperienced in travelling abroad, so the purpose is to broaden their experience of the travel and tourism industry.

Here are just three suggested activities in which your learners might be engaged:

• Planning various accommodation and itineraries aimed at different demographic groups based on the destination that you are visiting. The learners will visit those places while at the destination.

• Taking photographs while at the destination to display when back at school or college, perhaps as itineraries as above or cultural activities.

• Prior to travelling they may hold an introduction to the country they are visiting, experiencing food and culturally different music or languages.

Making the most of work-based learning as a teaching resource

The 2005, *14–19 Education and Skills* White Paper (DfES 2005) made work-related learning a compulsory element of the national curriculum, whereby all students at Key Stage 4 are required to take part in a two-week period of work experience, and this is further built into the new Diplomas as a part of the learner's commitment to applied learning.

The Department for Educations and Skills, in 2002 defined work experience or work-based learning (WBL) as: 'a placement on an employer's premises in which a learner carries out a particular task or duty, more or less as would an employee, but with the emphasis on the learning aspects of the experience' (quoted in DfES 2006: 24).

The process of delivering industry-related work experience again requires preparation and careful implementation if it is to be meaningful. The sustainability of employer involvement is crucial to accommodate the increase in demand that is being experienced in England. Your school or college may have access to organizations that place all the learners in a particular borough in placements or an in-house dedicated placement unit or department, but you will find your area Education Business Partnerships (EBP), another useful source of work placements. The national network of EBPs exists to make links between educational institutions and businesses and can be found in most regions. They will assist in finding employers willing to take learners on short-term placements: their website is www.ebp.org.

Planning learning and assessment around work-based learning

To make the most out of work-based learning, it is again essential that it is well planned and that the learners are fully prepared for the experience. For many it will be daunting and even disappointing since they will often be expected to carry out fairly menial tasks. But for younger learners there are a number of issues that limit what they can do. There may be legally imposed limits on the venues that they can enter and the kinds of tasks that they can perform. As we observed in Chapter 1, they may have ambitions to be travel agents, but stamping brochures does not fulfil their expectations.

However, in the better placements, they will be given the opportunity to shadow other employees to see what they do and, if they show initiative, may even be given fairly responsible tasks. As one teacher suggested, one of the most valuable outcomes from work experience for young people is to see how adults behave in the workplace.

The role of the teacher, then, is to plan the work-based learning experience to ensure that it meets the learning outcomes of the programme. The learning experience can focus on learning new skills; learning about the work environment, such as timekeeping and working in teams; or learning about one's self. Once the key objectives have been decided, the method of capturing the learning by assessment has to be planned.

Figure 6.5 suggests how this might be planned to good effect. It is based on a model developed for students in higher education, but we have adapted the principles for our purposes here.

Figure 6.6 is a summary of a BTEC National Unit designed to assess work experience. This will not only complement your planning but will also help to structure the learning experience for your students and enable them to gain credits for the study.

Preparation for work-based learning	• Understanding the workplace environment • Preparing a CV/application form • Practice interviews • Meeting the employers – interviews? • Research the placement work place • Expected behaviour
Developing WBL plans	• What are the learning outcomes? • How can they be achieved? • Understanding your role • Drawing up a learning plan • What do you hope to learn? • How will you record your learning experience?
Learners on WBL	• Experience regular tasks in the environment • Observe other workers' behaviour • Research other aspects of the environment • Keep a record of observations and tasks • Complete assignment tasks

Learners return from WBL	• Write up assignment tasks • Review WBL log record of activities • Share experiences with the group • Presentations on WBL? • Debrief • Self-assessment
Assessment and feedback	• Employer reports • Assessment of assignment and logbook • Feedback from peers and teacher • Next steps

Figure 6.5 Making the most of work-based learning (based on Graham's model 2004)

The following is a summary for this unit on work experience: it provides a structure for assessment to support the model shown in Figure 6.5.

1. **Know how to prepare for a work experience placement in the travel and tourism industry**
   Potential work placement organisations: e.g. travel agents and tour operators
   Contacts: e.g. tutors and careers advisors
   Other resources: e.g. newspapers, trade magazines and websites
   Constraints: e.g. location, travelling time and hours of work
   Complete documentation: e.g. letter of enquiry, letter of application and CV
   Set objectives: e.g. personal, career, curriculum

2. **Be able to demonstrate the skills, qualities and behaviours needed for effective performance in the workplace**
   Code of conduct: e.g. good timekeeping and attendance; accepting authority
   Demonstration of skills: e.g. social, technical and problem solving
   Monitoring progress: e.g. keeping own records and employer feedback

3. **Understand the nature of the chosen work experience organisation**
   Organisation type: e.g. ownership, sector, size and number of employees
   Organisation chart: e.g. type of structure and line management
   Key activities: e.g. tour operation, sales and provision of information
   Products and services: e.g. package holidays, insurance and accommodation
   Health and safety issues: e.g. legislative and regulatory requirements
   Own role: e.g. duties and responsibilities, and reporting structure
   Other staff roles: e.g. duties and responsibilities

4. **Understand the factors contributing to an effective work experience placement**
   Factors: e.g. skills development, attendance, punctuality, plans for future employment
   Supporting evidence: e.g. diary, logbook, employer feedback records, skills audit, witness statements

Figure 6.6 BTEC National content for Unit 21, Work Experience in the Travel and Tourism Industry

Apart from the planning and the monitoring of the experience, as with most learning, perhaps the most valuable aspect is the reflection and debrief afterwards to answer the question, 'What did you learn?' As we have suggested, this might best be achieved first through a presentation by the learner, and then by a plenary discussion between the whole group. Individual learners then can make up their minds as to how the experience has affected their perceptions of the industry and how it may have shaped their views on their own future.

Summary

In this final chapter we have tried to interpret 'resources' in the widest possible sense, but have been driven by our philosophy towards education in general, reflected in our earlier discussions of the curriculum. If we believe that the learners are at the centre of the process and we believe that learning is an interactive process, then our views on the resources we choose to use, as Morrison and Ridley (1989) pointed out, will tend to be 'first hand' and available to our learners. We will seek to fully engage them with resources that contextualize their learning in the world of travel and tourism and also in the world with which they are familiar, which may, of course, vary according to their own life experiences. For many though, this will mean a world of modern electronic media.

However, these resources are not merely ways of entertaining our learners, they must be carefully chosen to support and enhance their learning and to give it meaning. So they will give them the opportunity to experience first-hand aspects of travel and tourism whether experientially through work experience or taking part in activities in appropriate environments. To give credibility to our teaching of theory we can refer to a range of expert sources, from advanced texts to the vast number of video clips readily available.

Our role in all this is to ensure that we keep abreast of developments and manage these resources to make learning both a challenging and an enjoyable experience for our learners.

Appendix: Further reading and sources of information

Association of British Travel Agents: http://www.abta.com
Association of Independent Tour Operators: http://www.aito.co.uk/
Bray, R. and Raitz, V. (2001) *Flights to the Sun: The Story of the Holiday Revolution*. York: Continuum.
British Air Transport Association: http://www.bata.uk.com/Web/Default.aspx
Burns, P. and Novelli, M. (2007) *Tourism and Politics: Global Frameworks and Local Realities*. Oxford: Pergamon.
Civil Aviation Authority: http://www.caa.co.uk/
Cooper, C., Fletcher, J., Gilbert, D. and Fyall, A. (2008) *Tourism: Principles and Practice*. 4th edn. Harlow: Prentice Hall.
Department of Culture, Media and Sport (DCMS): http://www.culture.gov.uk
Discover Northern Ireland: http://www.discovernorthernireland.com/
National Air Traffic Control Services: http://www.nats.co.uk/6747/About-us.html
Oz Experience: http://www.ozexperience.com/
Page, S.J. (2007) *Tourism Management*. 2nd edn. Oxford: Butterworth-Heinemann.
People 1st: http://www.people1st.co.uk
Qualifications Assurance Agency for Higher Education: http://www.qaa.ac.uk/
Space Travel Virgin Galactic: http://www.virgingalactic.com/flash.html?language=english
Springboard UK: http://springboarduk.net/
The Tourism Alliance: http://www.tourismalliance.com/
Tourism Concern: http://www.tourismconcern.org.uk/index.php?page=about-us
Tourism Insights: http://www.insights.org.uk/
UK Boarder Agency: http://www.bia.homeoffice.gov.uk/
UK Identity and Passport Service: http://www.ips.gov.uk/cps/rde/xchg/ips_live/hs.xsl/index.htm
UKSP: http://www.uksp.co.uk/
Visit Britain: http://www.visitbritain.co.uk/
Visit Scotland: http://www.visitscotland.com/
Visit Wales: http://www.visitwales.co.uk/

Bibliography

Airey, D. (2005) 'Growth and development', in D. Airey and J. Tribe (eds), *An International Handbook of Tourism Education*. Oxford: Elsevier.

Airey, D. and Tribe, J. (2005) *An International Handbook of Tourism Education*. Oxford: Elsevier.

Appleyard, N. and Appleyard, K. (2009) *The Minimum Core for Language and Literacy*. Exeter: Learning Matters.

Armitage, A. and Renwick, M. (2008) *Assessment in FE*. London: Continuum.

Armitage, A., Bryant, R., Dunnill, R. et al. (2007) *Teaching and Training in Post-Compulsory Education*. 3rd edn. Maidenhead: Open University Press.

Bandura, A. (1969) *Social Learning and Personality Development*. London: Holt, Rinehart and Winston.

Biggs, J. (2007) *Teaching for Quality Learning at University*. Maidenhead: Open Univeristy Press.

Black, P. and Wiliam, D. (1998) *Inside the Black Box*. London: King's College.

Bloom, B. (1964) *Taxonomy of Educational Objectives: Handbook 1/Cognitive Domain*. London: Longman.

Brookfield, S. (1998) *Becoming Critically Reflective Teachers*. San Francisco, CA: Jossey-Bass.

Canwell, D. and Sutherland, J. (2003) *Student Book for AQA, OCR, WJEC and CCEA*. Cheltenham: Nelson Thornes.

Capel, S., Leask, M. and Turner, T. (2009) *Learning to Teach in the Secondary School*. 5th edn. Abingdon: Routledge.

Carden, C. (2009) *Classroom Activities for AQA GCSE Leisure & Tourism*. Llanrhystud: Travel and Tourism Publishing.

Clarke, A. (2006) *Teaching Adults ICT Skills*. Exeter: Learning Matters.

Coffield, F., Ecclestone, K., Hall, E. and Moseley, D. (2004) *Learning Styles and Pedagogy in Post-16 Learning. A Systematic and Critical Review*. London: LSRC.

Cooper, C., Wanhill, S., Fletcher, J., Gilbert, D. and Fayall, A. (2008) *Tourism: Principles and Practice*. 4th edn. Harlow: Prentice Hall Financial Times.

Delaney, J. (2009) 'Minimum core – language/literacy'. Unpublished paper, Canterbury Christ Church University, Canterbury.

Department for Culture, Media and Sport (DCMS) (1999) *Tomorrow's Tourism*. London: DCMS.

Department for Culture, Media and Sport (DCMS) (2005) *Winning: A Tourism Strategy for 2012 and Beyond*. London: HMSO.

Department for Education and Employment (DfEE) (1996) *Review of Qualifications for 16–19 Year Olds*. Dearing Report. London: DfEE.

Department for Education and Employment (DfEE) (1999) *A Fresh Start: Improving Literacy and Numeracy*. Moser Report. London: DfEE.

Department for Education and Employment (DfEE) (2000) *Foundation Degree: A Consultation Paper*. London: DfEE.

Department for Education and Employment (DfEE) (2006) *Prosperity for All in the Global Economy – World Class Skills*. Leitch Report. Norwich: HMSO.

Department for Education and Skills (DfES) (2004) *Improving Differentiation in Business Education*. London: DfES.

Department for Education and Skills (DfES) (2005) *14–19 Education and Skills*. White Paper. London: HMSO.

Department for Education and Skills (DfES) (2006) 'Work experience: a guide for employers', in *Work-Related Learning and the Law: Guidance for Schools and School-Business Link Practitioners*. http://publications.teachernet.gov.uk/eOrderingDownload/DFES-0340-2006.pdf (accessed 30 April 2010).

Department for Education and Skills and the Qualifications and Curriculum Authority (DfES and QCA) (1999) *Aims for the School Curriculum*. London: HMSO.

Department for Education and Skills (DfES) Standards Unit (2004) *Improving Differentiation in Business Education*. London: DfES.

Dewey, J. (1963) *Experience and Education*. New York: Collier.

Dewey, J. (1974) *John Dewey on Education: Selected Writings*. Chicago, IL: University of Chicago Press.

Donovan, G. (2005) *Teaching 14–19*. London: David Fulton.

Edexcel (2007) *Specifications Level 3 BTEC Nationals in Travel and Tourism*. London: Edexcel.

Fegas, A. and Nicoll, K. (2008) *Foucault and Lifelong Learning*. Abingdon: Routledge.

Flemming, N.D. (2001) *Teaching and Learning Styles: VARK Strategies*. New Zealand: N.D. Flemming.

Freire, P. (1970) *Pedagogy of the Oppressed*. London: Continuum.

Gibbs, G. (1992) *Improving the Quality of Student Learning*. Plymouth: Technical and Educational Services.

Graham, J. (2004) 'Reflective portfolios for work-based learning'. www.heacademy.ac.uk/assets/hlst/documents/LINK.Newsletter/Link11 (accessed 7 Feb. 2010).

Green, A. and Lucas, N. (1999) 'Repositioning further education: a sector for the twenty-first century', in A. Green and N. Lucas (eds), *F.E. and Lifelong Learning: Realigning the Sector for the Twenty-First Century*. London: University of London, Institute of Education.

Green Paper (2007) *Raising Expectations*. London: HMSO.

Hargreaves, D., Hestar, S. and Mellor, F. (1975) *Deviance in Classrooms*. London: Routledge and Kegan Paul.

Harkin, J.T., Turner, G. and Dawn, T. (2001) *Teaching Young Adults*. London: Routledge Falmer.

Hodgson, A. and Spours, K. (2003) *Beyond A Levels Curriculum 2000 and the Reform of 14–19 Qualifications*. London: Routledge Falmer.

Honey, P. and Mumford, A. (1992) *The Manual of Learning Styles*. Maidenhead: P. Honey.

Horrocks, J.E. (1976) *The Psychology of Adolescence*. Boston, MA: Houghton Mifflin.

Hyland, T. (1994) *Competence, Education and NVQs: Dissenting Perspectives*. London: Cassell.

Hyland, T. and Merrill, B. (2003) *The Changing Face of Further Education*. Abingdon: Routledge.

Jaques, D. and Salmon, G. (2007) *Learning in Groups*. 4th edn. London: Routledge.

Knowles, M. (1984) *The Adult Learner, a Neglected Species*. 3rd edn. Houston, TX: Gulf.

Kolb, D.A. (1984) *Experiential Learning: Experience as the Source of Learning and Development*. London: Prentice Hall.

Lea, J., Armitage, A., Hayes, D., Lomas, L. and Markless, S. (2003) *Working in Post-Compulsory Education*. Maidenhead: Open University Press.

Leiper, N. (1995) 'Tourism systems: an interdisciplinary perspectives', Department of Management Systems Occasional Paper 2, Massey University, Palmerston North.

Lumby, J. and Foskett, N. (2005) *14–19 Education: Policy, Leadership and Learning*. London: Sage.

McDonald, J.P. (1992) 'Dilemmas of planning backwards: rescuing a good idea', *Teachers' College Record*, 94: 152–69.

Morrison, K. and Ridley, K. (1989) 'Curriculum ideologies' in M. Preedy (ed.) *Approaches to Curriculum Management*. Milton Keynes: Open University Press.

Nasta, T. (1994) *How to Design a Vocational Curriculum*. London: Kogan Page.

Page, S.J. (2007) *Tourism Management: Managing for Change*. 2nd edn. Oxford: Butterworth-Heinemann.

Peart, S. (2009) *The Minimum Core for Numeracy*. Exeter: Learning Matters.

People 1st (2007) *National Skills Strategy: Raising the Bar*. Uxbridge: People 1st.

Petty, G. (2004) *Teaching Today: A Practical Guide*. 3rd edn. Cheltenham: Nelson Thornes.

Petty, G. (2006) *Evidence Based Teaching: A Practical Approach*. Cheltenham: Nelson Thornes.

Petty, G. (2009) *Teaching Today*. 4th edn. Cheltenham: Nelson Thornes.

Qualifications and Curriculum Authority (QCA) (2005) 'A review of GCE and GCSE coursework arrangements'. www.qca.org.uk/15525.html (accessed 8 Feb. 2010).

Qualifications and Curriculum Authority (QCA) (2007) *Functional Skills Standards*. London: QCA.

Qualifications and Curriculum Development Agency (QCDA) (2009) Literacy, Numeracy and the Key Skills. http://www.qcda.gov.uk/4537.aspx: (accessed 21 Oct. 2009).

Race, P. and Pickford, R. (2007) *Making Teaching Work*. London: Sage.

Reece, I. and Walker, S. (2007) *Teaching, Training and Learning: A Practical Guide*. 6th edn. Sunderland: Business Education Publications.

Richards, G. (2007) *Cultural Tourism: Global and Local Perspectives*. Binghampton, NY: Haworth Hospitality Press.

Royal Society for the Prevention of Accidents (ROSPA) (2001) *Safety Education*. London: ROSPA. Also available at: http://www.rospa.com/SafetyEducation/AdviceAnd Information/Health-And-Safety-At-School/SchoolTrips/out-and-about.aspx

Savage, J. (2008) *Teenage: The Creation of Youth Culture*. London: Pimlico.

SPRITO (1997) *Coaching, Teaching and Instructing: National Occupational Standards Level 2. S/NVQ Guide*. London: SPRITO.

Stenhouse, L. (1975) *An Introduction to Curriculum Research and Development*. London: Heinemann.

The City and Guilds of London (2005) *Level 3 NVQ in Tourism and Travel Services – Standards and Assessment Requirements*. London: City and Guilds of London.

The Treasury Office (2003) *Every Child Matters*. London: HMSO.

Thomas, S., Smees, R., Macbeath, J. and Robertson, P. (2000) 'Valuing pupils' views in Scottish schools', *Educational Research and Evaluation*, 6(4): 281–316.

Tribe, J. (2005) 'Tourism, knowledge and the curriculum', in D. Airey and J. Tribe (eds), *An International Handbook of Tourism Education*. Oxford: Elsevier.

Tummons, J. (2007) *Assessing Learning in the Lifelong Learning Sector.* Exeter: Learning Matters.

Tyler, R. (1971) *Basic Principles for Curriculum and Instruction.* Chicago, IL: University of Chicago Press.

Vygotsky, L.S. (1962) *Thought and Language.* Cambridge, MA: Harvard University Press.

Wallace, S. (2005) *Teaching and Supporting Learning in Further Education: Meeting the FENTO Standards.* Exeter: Learning Matters.

Weston, P. (1992) 'A decade for differentiation', *British Journal of Special Education,* 19(1): 21.

Wiggins, G.P. (1993) *Assessing Student Performance.* San Francisco, CA: Jossey-Bass.

Wolf, A. (2000) *Competency Based Assessment.* Buckingham: Open University Press.

Working Group on 14–19 Reform (2004) *14–19 Curriculum and Qualifications Reform.* Tomlinson Report. Norwich: HMSO.

Websites

http://www.apprenticeships.org.uk

http://www.caa.co.uk/default.aspx?catid=286

https://cityandguilds.com/documents/ind_travel/SP-02-4847.pdf

https://www.cruiseservices.co.uk/the-cruise-industry.html

http://dcsf.gov.uk/everychildmatters

http://dcsf.gov.uk/furthereducation

http://www.ebp.org

http://www.edexcel.com/migrationdocuments/BTEC%20Nationals/
    315894_BN018369_NACD_in_Travel_and_Tourism_L3_Issue_2.pdf

http://www.edexcel.com/quals/Pages/qual-home.aspx

http://heacademy.ac.uk/hist/ourwork/heinfe/teachingexchange

http://www.insights.org.uk/

http://www.literacytrust.org.uk/socialinclusion/youngpeople/1419paper

http://www.nocn.org.uk/about-us/mission%2c-vision-and-values

http://www.qcda.gov.uk/4534.aspx

http://www.reblackpool.com/.

http://www.rospa.com/safetyeducation/schooltrips/part2.htm

http://www.skillsactive.com/training/apprenticeships/young-apprenticeships

http://stile.coventry.ac.uk/cbs/staff/beech/tourism

http://www.tourismtrade.org.uk/MarketIntelligenceResearch/KeyTourismFacts.asp:

http://www.uksp.co.uk/CareerMap.aspx

www.untwo.org/index.php

http://www.visitliverpool.com/merseywise/home

www.world-tourism.org

Index

Related books from Open University Press

Purchase from www.openup.co.uk or order through your local bookseller

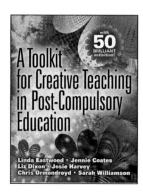

A TOOLKIT FOR CREATIVE TEACHING IN POST-COMPULSORY EDUCATION

Linda Eastwood, Jennie Coates, Liz Dixon, Josie Harvey, Chris Ormondroyd and Sarah Williamson

978-0-335-23416-5 (Paperback)
2009

eBook also available

This is the essential resource for trainees and teachers working in the PCET sector who are looking for new and creative ways of engaging and motivating their learners.

Key features:

- 50 practical and innovative teaching activities
- Variations and subject-specific examples
- Thinking Points to encourage reflection
- A theoretical framework which sets the activities within the context of creativity and innovation

www.openup.co.uk

OPEN UNIVERSITY PRESS
McGraw · Hill Education

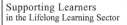

SUPPORTING LEARNERS IN THE LIFELONG LEARNING SECTOR

Marilyn Fairclough

978-0-335-23362-5 (Paperback)
2009

eBook also available

This is the first book of its kind to deal with the topic of supporting learners in PCET, rather than just focusing on how to teach them.

Key features:

- Each chapter cross-referenced to the QTLS Professional Standard for those on PTLLS, CTLLS and DTLLS courses
- Real life examples from a variety of settings and subjects
- Practical suggestions for developing classroom practice
- Suggestions for managing disruptive behaviour

www.openup.co.uk

OPEN UNIVERSITY PRESS
McGraw - Hill Education

**MODELS OF LEARNING,
TOOLS FOR TEACHING
Third Edition**

Bruce Joyce, Emily Calhoun
and David Hopkins

978-0-335-23419-6 (Paperback)
2008

eBook also available

This bestselling text provides a comprehensive and accessible
introduction to an array of models of teaching and learning.

Key features:

- A new chapter on teaching adolescents with disabilities to read
- A wealth of new scenarios and examples with clear guidelines for
  implementation
- New research and illustrations
- A revised Picture Word Inductive Model

www.openup.co.uk

OPEN UNIVERSITY PRESS
McGraw - Hill Education